TIMELESS MYTHS

THE NATIVE AMERICANS

◈ *a beginner's guide* ◈

STEVE EDDY

Hodder & Stoughton
A MEMBER OF THE HODDER HEADLINE GROUP

Acknowledgements

I would like to thank the following for their knowledge, help and hospitality: Carlyle Antonio of the American Indian Trust, Bristol; Larry De Coteau; Chris Hall and his pupils as St Joseph's Indian School, Chamberlain; Alta Cable; Clark (Blue Bird) Zephier; Floyd (Looks for Buffalo) Hand and family; Reg Red Hoop and Chris at the Walakota Waldorf School, and Lula Red Cloud (whose medicine wheel has been on my desk throughout the writing of this book).

Every effort has been made to contact the holders of copyright material but if any have been inadvertently overlooked, the publisher will be pleased to make the necessary alterations at the first opportunity.

Order queries: please contact Bookpoint Ltd, 39 Milton Park, Abingdon, Oxon OX14 4TD. Telephone: (44) 01235 827720, Fax: (44) 01235 400454. Lines are open from 9.00–6.00, Monday to Saturday, with a 24-hour message answering service.
Email address: orders@bookpoint.co.uk

British Library Cataloguing in Publication Data
A catalogue record for this title is available from The British Library

ISBN 0 340 77227 1

First published 2000
Impression number   10 9 8 7 6 5 4 3 2 1
Year   2005 2004 2003 2002 2001 2000

Copyright © 2000 Steve Eddy

All rights reserved. No part of this publication may be reproduced or transmitted in any form or by any means, electronic or mechanical, including photocopy, recording, or any information storage and retrieval system, without permission in writing from the publisher or under licence from the Copyright Licensing Agency Limited. Further details of such licences (for reprographic reproduction) may be obtained from the Copyright Licensing Agency Limited, of 90 Tottenham Court Road, London W1P 9HE.

Typeset by Transet Ltd, Coventry, England.
Printed in Great Britain for Hodder & Stoughton Educational, a division of Hodder Headline Plc, 338 Euston Road, London NW1 3BH by Cox & Wyman.

Contents

Chapter 1	Who are the Native Americans?	1
Chapter 2	Origins	5
	Lakota creation	5
	Hopi creation	7
	Other myths	11
	Application	13
Chapter 3	Our place on earth	14
	The Six Grandfathers	14
	The directions within	16
	Sacred sites	17
	Earth and stars	19
	Application	24
Chapter 4	The spirit world and nature	25
	Archetypes	26
	Respect for nature	27
	Time and timelessness	29
	Visitors from the spirit world	31
	Crying for a vision	32
	Divination	34
	Application	35
Chapter 5	Symbolism and the arts	36
	Sacred architecture	36
	Sacred art	38
	Power or supersitition?	42
	Application	44
Chapter 6	Gateways	45
	Birth and childhood	46
	Puberty and marriage	49
	The spirit journey	51
	Application	54
Chapter 7	The turning wheel	56
	The nature and purpose of ritual	56
	Common elements in ritual	57
	The sacred pipe	59
	The sweatlodge	61
	The seasons	63
	The Sundance	67

	Personal rituals	68
	The giveaway	69
	The Ghost dance	70
	Application	71
Chapter 8	Codes of conduct	73
	Speaking from the heart	74
	Whose land?	76
	The warrior code	77
	The role of women	78
	Old and young	79
	Socializing and hospitality	81
	Demoncracy	81
	Application	82

Conclusions	83
References	85
Bibliography	87
Index	89

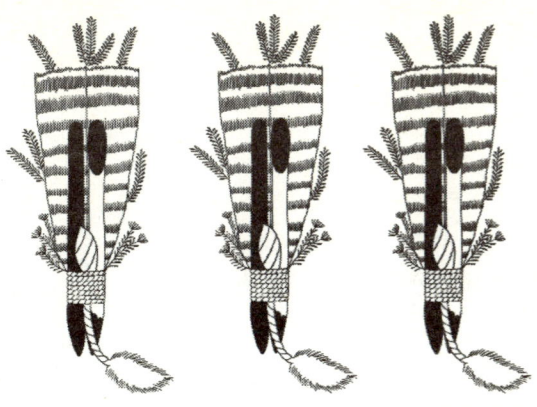

Chapter 1
Who are the Native Americans?

One does not sell the earth upon which the people walk.
[Crazy Horse, Lakota]

The first Native Americans probably arrived on the continent in waves of migration from Siberia between 10,000 and 20,000 years ago. Archaeologists believe that most crossed the Bering Straits, once a land bridge, until a warmer climate caused the ice caps to melt and sea levels to rise. Some interesting but controversial evidence, in archaeology and myth, suggests that tribes such as the Hopi may have crossed the South Pacific to arrive on the south-west coast, and that others may have colonized South America and then moved north.

Certainly by 10,000 years ago most of North America was populated. There were several hundred tribes, speaking diverse languages falling into several large groups, including Algonquin, Athapascan, Caddo, Iroquoian and Siouan. Linguistic connections between now-distant tribes, such as the Koyukon of north-west Canada and the Navajo and Apache of the south-west, show that vast migrations must have taken place within the continent.

The first Europeans to arrive, and perhaps to intermarry, were the Vikings, whose *Vinland Sagas* describe the 'skraelings' they encountered. Columbus arrived in 1492, and it is his geographical blunder that gave the indigenous people the name 'Indians'. A steady trickle of European explorers and adventurers ensued. In 1500 the Portuguese Gaspar Corte-Real reached Labrador (north-east Canada) and the following year kidnapped two shiploads of natives as slaves – setting an example that was followed by other whites, though not with great success.

Over the next two centuries, the Spanish concentrated on the south and the English and French on the north. Coronado led an army from Mexico into the Plains, lured by tales of a fabulous city of gold, and committed atrocities against the Hopi, Zuni and Pueblo. De Soto, who presented himself as 'the child of the Sun', was worse. A Spanish campaign of 1595 led by Onante and Zaldivar was similarly barbaric.

When whites settled in the east, they found the locals welcoming and helpful. There were many instances of communities that would not have survived without practical Native help. Sadly, the pattern was for friendliness to turn to suspicion and hostility as the settlers demanded more and more from their hosts, especially when they sought exclusive rights to tribal lands.

As immigration increased and the white population exploded, Native Americans were driven ever westwards, or survived in pockets of undesirable or inaccessible land, such as the Florida swamps. Many tribes were wiped out by European diseases. The Pilgrim Fathers (English Puritans who formed a colony in the seventeenth century) were probably saved by a Patuxet called Squanto, but his tribe were killed by plague. This trend continued into the late nineteenth century. Most of the Mandan tribe died of smallpox in 1837.

The forced relocations of Native Americans by the US Government throughout the nineteenth century had a devastating effect: peoples driven from their homes sickened and died by the thousand – not just from the hardships of travel, or starvation, but from the heartache of being torn from their spiritual homeland. President Andrew Jackson forced the Choctaw from Mississippi to Oklahoma in 1830–1833. Observers reported their grief, and that many of them reached out and touched the trees before turning to leave. Another case was that of the Cherokee, most of whom were forced to emigrate from their south-eastern homeland to the west in 1835.

There was valiant resistance, but by the second half of the nineteenth century the Plains formed the last refuge of the free Native American. The Apache, led by Geronimo, did not surrender until 1886. In the north, the Lakota continued to beat off the white man, notably eliminating General Custer and the Seventh Cavalry at Little Big Horn in 1876 (an event referred to by the Lakota as, 'the Rubbing Out of Long Hair' in reference to Custer's famous locks).

Lakota resistance continued even after they had lost their sacred Black Hills. Soon a new religion was to bring hope, even though most were now confined to reservations. The 'Ghost dance' was a peaceful movement intended to bring about a removal of the white man and renewal of the land by ritual dance and song (see page 70). In December 1890, a thousand or more Lakota danced on Stronghold Table, a flat-topped eminence, still awe-inspiringly empty, which drops off dramatically into the eerie, parched landscape of the Badlands. Here and elsewhere, the sight of huge numbers of Indians dancing for days and nights on end unnerved the federal agents. They heard rumours of an intended revolt, probably compounded by stories of the widespread belief among the Indians that their painted 'ghost shirts' were bullet-proof.

The authorities started to round up 'trouble-makers'. Sitting Bull, who was not even a Ghost dancer, came peaceably but died when shooting broke out. Many of his band fled, about a hundred joining Big Foot's band of Minneconjou Lakota. A warrant was issued for Big Foot's arrest. When he learned of Sitting Bull's death, he started to move his band towards Pine Ridge Reservation in the hope of gaining the protection of Chief Red Cloud there.

With snow now falling, the Seventh Cavalry pursued Big Foot's band through the harsh terrain of the Badlands, Big Foot now sick with pneumonia. When the cavalry caught up, Big Foot surrendered. The cavalry escorted the band of 120 men and 230 women and children towards Pine Ridge. They stopped to camp at Wounded Knee, the cavalry's powerful Hotchkiss guns trained on them from a nearby hill. When the soldiers disarmed the band, somehow a rifle went off. Instantly, the soldiers began to fire into the now largely unarmed Lakotas, quickly backed up by the Hotchkiss guns. Around 300 Lakota were killed, and 25 soldiers.

Medicine man Black Elk said that at Wounded Knee a dream died, and the sacred hoop of the people was broken. There followed grim years of semi-starvation, compulsory government schooling, with Native children forbidden to speak their own language, the banning of ceremonies – the wilful destruction of a whole culture.

Fortunately, while much was lost, much wisdom was preserved by elders and passed down. Some ceremonies were revived by recourse to anthropological texts. Nowadays, Native American culture and spirituality is gaining in strength, along with political moves to secure land and gain compensation. While tribal practices continue, a kind of pan-Nativism has emerged, focusing on the ways of the Plains tribes, especially the Lakota. (The Lakota are the biggest dialect group of the 'Sioux', who prefer the generic name Lakota, as 'Sioux' actually means 'treacherous snakes' in the Ojibway language.)

Reservation communities are still poor, and there is still a feeling of disenfranchisement – as well as alcoholism, domestic violence and ill health. However, casinos are, ironically, helping to bring money in, and there is growing support for traditional ways, as well as a recognition by Europeans that Native American wisdom has much to offer our spiritually disconnected, environmentally challenged industrial societies. Here and elsewhere in the rest of the book, the term 'Europeans' refers to those of European descent, including non-Native Americans, and anyone brought up in European-based culture.

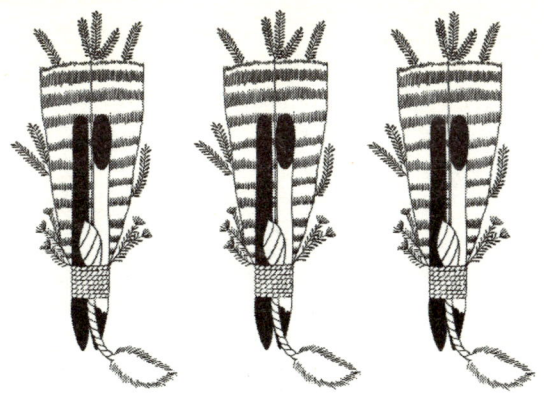

Chapter 2
Origins

It makes no difference as to the name of God, since love is the real God of all the world.

[Apache]

Most Native Americans feel a need to know their personal ancestry – to know where they come from. It is a natural extension of this to want to establish the origins of the tribe as a whole, of humanity, of life and earth, and of the universe. It follows that a large proportion of Native American myths are about these origins. Some, for example, the widespread tales of a great flood, may be based on ancient events, but whether or not they are taken as literal truth, they certainly embody psychological truths. Moreover, these truths are underlined by the striking resemblance that many Native American myths bear to myths from other cultures. Flood myths are one example; tales of stealing fire – reminiscent of the Greek myth of Prometheus – are another.

Lakota creation

According to Lakota myth, in the beginning was Inyan – rock. He was shapeless and omnipresent, and his spirit was Wakan Tanka – the Great Mystery. Han also existed in some sense, but not as a being – only as a darkness. Inyan longed to exercise his powers – or in some versions of the myth his compassion – but lacked anything on which to do this. He knew that if there were to be another, he would have to create it from himself, giving it spirit and a part of his own blue blood. He decided to create this other as part of himself in order to keep control of his powers. Therefore he created a great disc whose border was as the limits of space, to become Mother Earth, naming her Maka. But in making her he sacrificed his blood, which became the waters, and he shrivelled up and became hard and lost some of his power.

Since the water could not retain the power, it went into the making of Skan, the blue dome of the sky. Maka, meanwhile, complained to Inyan that all was cold and dark, so Inyan created Anp, the red light. This was not enough for her, so Inyan created Wi, the sun. Maka was still not satisfied: she wanted to be separate, not part of her creator. Inyan, however, had expended all his power, and could only appeal to Skan, in his role as supreme judge. Skan ruled that Maka had to stay bound up with Inyan – which is why rocks are bound up with soil.

In another version, Inyan loses all his power when he makes Maka, and she taunts him with his impotence, so that he appeals to Skan. Skan then banishes Han – darkness – and creates Anp to light the world. When Maka complains that she is still cold, Skan creates Wi, the sun. Apparently hard to please, Maka now complains that she is too hot. Skan therefore orders Han and Anp to follow each other round the world, thus creating day and night.

To the Lakota, the most significant part of the myth, in either version, is Inyan's self-sacrifice in making the world, and it is this sacrifice that is celebrated in the Sundance (see page 67). It is interesting that in Lakota creation, as in some other Native American creation myths, such as that of the Hopi (see below), the prime mover of the universe is motivated by a desire to interact, and has to create another, more dynamic deity to continue creation. Duality, represented by day and night, is considered an essential part of this creation. Skan, Father Sky, resembles the Greek Zeus, and even creates for himself a daughter, the beautiful Wohpe, patron of beauty, harmony and pleasure. This sounds very like the Greek Aphrodite, daughter of Zeus. Perhaps the message is that harmony springs from judgement.

In Lakota myth there are other lesser gods, but all of the gods are perceived as being part of Wakan Tanka. This essential unity and mystery of godhead is a feature that is common to all Native American belief.

Hopi creation

The Hopi creation myth begins with Taiowa – the Creator – residing in Tokpela – Endless Space. Taiowa, the infinite, conceived of the finite and created Sotuknang to manifest his plans for life in Endless Space. Following Taiowa's instructions, Sotuknang gathered together whatever was to be given substance, and arranged it into nine universes: one for Taiowa, one for himself, and seven for the life to come. Then Taiowa told him to make each universe half solid and half water, to make the winds, and to create life.

In order to create life, Sotuknang, went to Tokpela – the First World – and out of it he created Spider Woman. 'Why am I here?' she asked. Sotuknang told her that she had been given the power to create life, and following his instructions she mixed some earth with saliva and created twin beings. Then she wrapped them in a blanket of creative wisdom, and sang the Song of Creation over them to bring them to life. To Poqaghoya, on her right, she gave the task of solidifying the earth; to Palongawhoya, on her left, she gave the task of sending out sound to activate the vibratory centres along the earth's axis, so that everything was attuned to Tiowa and sang his praises. Then she sent Poqaghoya to the North Pole and his twin to the South, instructing them to keep the earth turning on its axis.

Now that the earth was ready to receive life, Spider Woman made all the plants and animals. Finally she mixed yellow, red, white and black earth with saliva to make four men, and then made them partners in her own image. Finally she asked Sotuknang to give them the powers of speech and reproduction, which he did, giving each colour of man a different language.

These first people lived in a paradise, understanding perfectly the mystery of their divine parenthood. They also understood that a human body was like the earth; it had an axis, its spine, along which were seven vibratory centres which echoed the primal sound of the universe and warned if anything was wrong.

These centres correspond closely in concept to the *chakras* of Hindu belief. If the Hopi are correct, then our human energy centres correspond to those of our planet. According to the Hopi, before evil entered the world there was no sickness, but after it did, a shaman could tell what was wrong with a patient by laying his hands on these vibratory centres.

All was well, until people began to forget their divine origins and to use their vibratory centres for earthly purposes. Then a trouble-maker came, the Talker, in the form of Mochni, a bird. He talked and talked, convincing the people of the differences among themselves, and between them and the animals. The guardian spirit of the animals made them afraid of man. Then, to make matters worse, there came Katoya, the Beguiler, in the form of a handsome snake. He sowed seeds of suspicion, so that people began to accuse each other, and eventually to make war.

This First World had clearly become corrupt, and Sotuknang and Taiowa decided to destroy it and start again. However, they observed that a few people were still virtuous. Sotuknang told them that the vibratory centre at the top of their heads (the crown chakra, in Hindu thought) would guide them to a place from where they would be able to follow a cloud by day and a star by night. They did this. Some people could not see the cloud and star, but took the message on trust. They were all guided to an anthill. Sotuknang told them that the Ant People would look after them, and that they were to learn from the Ant People's industry, foresight and harmony. He then destroyed the world by fire, since the first people had been led by the Fire Clan.

Sotuknang now created a Second World, not quite as lovely as the first. The people had learned to store food like the ants, so they had a surplus to barter for goods. But trade led to disagreements and fighting, and so Taiowa and Sotuknang decided to destroy this world too, again guiding a chosen few to take refuge with the Ant People. This time the world was destroyed by water and ice when the Twins abandoned the Poles and the earth spun off-balance.

Sotuknang created a Third World, and once again the people emerged from the underworld. Sotuknang warned them to respect him, and each other, and to sing praises to Taiowa from the mountain tops. After a while there was a population explosion and people began to live in cities, where it was difficult to sing praises. Many people began to abuse the power of sexuality. Worse, some made shields of hide on which they flew through the air to attack other cities.

This time Sotuknang told Spider Woman to save the virtuous few in hollow reeds, and then flooded the earth. Eventually the survivors found themselves on an island that had been their highest peak. They sent out birds to look for land, but Sotuknang told them through Spider Woman to make boats and paddle north-east. They journeyed on as directed, stopping off at bigger and bigger islands, until they came to the 'Place of Emergence' on the American continent – the Fourth World. Sotuknang showed them the islands, saying: 'They are the footprints of your journey.' Then he sank them.

Hopi Mother Earth symbols

This Fourth World – our present world – was the most materialistic and degraded so far. Even so, it was beautiful, though less so than its predecessor. Its guardian spirit, Másaw, told the people that they were on the backbone of the new world (probably the Rockies), and he gave them four tablet depicting the paths of the migrations on which they must go. Each clan had to migrate in each of the four directions in turn. Over what one must assume was a matter of several thousand years, the clans did this, some losing sight of their purpose and settling down, others continuing towards the area in the South-West that is now Hopi territory. As they turned at each extremity, their migratory path formed a swastika, either sunwise or earthwise (see page 9). This process of emergence is expressed in rock pictographs in two forms of the Mother Earth symbol, the central cross showing the four directions.

This Hopi myth has some compelling implications. First, it could be taken literally. The series of worlds, each one destroyed in turn, is reminiscent of the *yugas* ('great ages') of Hindu belief. In both cases, successive worlds are associated with the same increasingly base metals: gold, silver, copper, and mixed mineral (Hopi) or iron (Hindu). A difference, however, is that in the Hopi myth this Fourth World is not the last in the present series, as it will be followed by another three. Each series of seven worlds will pass through the seven universes – a total of 49 worlds. Both Hopi and Hindu myths can be related to one version of the astrophysicists' Big Bang Theory, according to which, we live in a pulsating universe which on a cosmic timescale passes through repeated cycles. In each cycle, the universe begins with matter infinitely compressed (like the Lakota's Inyan); it then 'explodes', expanding for millions of years until it reaches the point at which gravity outweighs this momentum, when the universe starts to contract, so that eventually a new cycle begins.

There may have been worlds destroyed by fire, and destruction by water and ice might occur as a result of the earth spinning off its axis in the event of colliding with another body. As for destruction by flood, there are so many mythical parallels, from Genesis to Atlantis, that we must at least consider the idea that this may have actually happened. Moreover, global warming threatens to make this a new reality, at least for low-lying areas. The saving of the chosen few from a corrupt world is a widespread mythical and religious idea. Could it contain literal truth?

The Hopi's account of their 'emergence' is fascinating historically, too. Most archaeologists say that the first Native Americans entered the continent via the Bering Straits. But the Hopi myth makes a case for at least some immigrants arriving via the Pacific. There is some evidence for their extensive migrations, too, in the form of rock carvings. Moreover, there are ceremonial, mythical and artistic similarities between the Hopi and the Toltecs, Mayas and Aztecs, all of whom the Hopi believe to have been Hopi clans who failed to complete their migrations.

On the other hand, myths of emergence from the underworld – shared by many tribes – could suggest the evolutionary development of human consciousness. Similarly, the flood motif could point to inundation of the conscious mind by the unconscious, and the gradual re-emergence of the conscious.

Other myths

Several tribes in addition to the Hopi have myths of an emergence from the underworld. A Lakota myth tells how the tribe lived underground until the evil Iktome, Spider Man, sent Wolf to tempt them out onto the surface by reports of how easy life was there. They ignored the warnings of the holy man Tatanka and emerged through Wind Cave in the Black Hills. Tatanka then sacrificed himself by becoming a buffalo in order to feed them.

A Jicarilla Apache myth tells of emergence from a world underground and underwater. The Sun looks through a hole and spies another world up above, and so the people build mounds of earth in the four directions and plant them with fruits. The mounds grow to be mountains and, with the help of a ladder made from the right horns of obliging buffalo, the people climb out onto the world. Storms roll away the waters, allowing the people to travel in each of the four directions in turn until they reach the sea – reminding us of the Hopi migrations.

Linguistic similarities between the Apache and north-western tribes suggest that in historical terms they actually migrated across the Bering Straits, arriving in their present homeland much later than other tribes in the area, such as the Hopi and Zuni – around the end of the first millennium. Their Navajo neighbours are closely related to them and probably arrived around the same time. The Navajo creation story, told in a two-day Blessingway ceremony, tells how First Man and First Woman emerged into this world near Huerfano Mountain in New Mexico. First Man found a baby girl on an adjacent mountain. She grew up in four days, to become Changing Woman, and created the four original clans from her body. Her son rid the Navajo lands of monsters and made them safe for the people to inhabit.

A myth of the Caddo, a tribe from what is now eastern Texas, strikingly resembles the story of the biblical Noah. Four strange children grow into monsters that threaten to destroy the world. A wise man hears a voice telling him: 'I will create a great flood. Plant a hollow reed in the ground. When it grows, climb into it with your wife, taking a pair of each of the good animals with you, and you will all be saved.' The man asks for a warning sign and is told to watch for a great flock of birds. This comes, and he climbs into the reed with his wife and the animals. Then the voice says: 'I will send Turtle to destroy the monsters.' Turtle does this by undermining the monsters and drowning them, thus creating the four directions.

The Turtle also features in an Ojibway myth, saving the world from flood by swimming down and coming up with enough earth on his back to form the American continent. Here we see again the theme of self-sacrifice, since the Turtle drowns. Many tribes now refer to North America as 'Turtle Island', and turtles are a popular subject for the stone carvings at which the Ojibway are particularly skilled.

Similarly, in an Iroquois myth the Sky God's daughter is pushed through a hole in the sky into a flooded world, but is saved when water fowl persuade the Turtle to help her. Toad dives for mud and piles it up on Turtle's back to make the land. Another Iroquois myth introduces the idea of good and evil. According to this account, Sky Woman was impregnated by Earth Holder and fell to earth, where she gave birth to Great Spirit and Evil Spirit. When Sky Woman died, Great Spirit sent her head into the sun, and her body into the moon and stars. He then created life on earth. Evil Spirit was banished, but still tries to create conflict and disorder.

Application

'Wisdom' in the Micmac language is *unkecdasee wach'n*: 'the state of thinking big thoughts'. Creation myths are especially potent in creating these 'big thoughts'. On one level they satisfy a human need for explanations; on another they encapsulate unfathomable truths about our fundamental origins.

Consider the implications of the Lakota and Hopi creation stories, coupled with the Big Bang Theory. In all three, the universe begins from a single source. In the Lakota myth, Inyan – rock – is spirit made solid. Within this there is an urge towards expansion and diversification, as there must have been to bring about the astrophysicists' 'Big Bang'. Everything you see around you has stemmed from this moment, this point of unity. Everything bears the memory of this first unity. You and all other individual points of consciousness come from this source.

To focus on this imaginatively, contemplate a rock. Imagine it as the primal unity. Become aware of its density and solidity, and of the energy locked up in it – energy that includes you. Think of it as the Lakota would – as Inyan. What does it tell you?

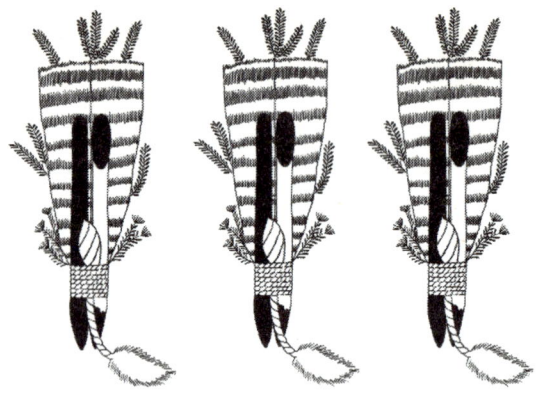

Chapter 3
Our place on earth

The Crow country is in exactly the right place.

[Crow]

The Six Grandfathers

Like several other peoples across the world, including the Celts and the ancient Chinese, most Native American tribes orientate themselves according to the directions. To the Celts there were four – north, east, south and west – and sometimes a fifth – centre. To Native Americans there are usually six: the four points of the compass, together with above and below – heaven and earth. Each of these has special powers, qualities and associations. Those outlined below are for the Lakota.

West

The west is where thunderclouds and rain come from. Water is associated with life, renewal and purification. It is used in purification rituals such as the sweatlodge (see page 61). The west is ruled by the Wakinyan, the powerful winged Thunder Beings. It is also sometimes associated with destruction, though in the cosmic scheme of things this is not necessarily a bad thing. The Lakota call the path of self-destruction – for example, of alcoholism – the Black Road, and the colour of the west is black. The Horse People, with their thundering hooves, live in the west, but the messenger of the west is the black thunderbird.

North

The north is the home of winter, but its power brings health and personal growth through self-discipline and endurance. It is the home of the Buffalo Nation (Tatanka Oyate) and of the White Buffalo Calf Woman who brought the Lakota their sacred pipe and rituals. It is also the place inhabited by Waziah, the unpredictable giant who in modern Lakota consciousness has merged with Father Christmas. The colour of the north is red, and to live a good life in tune with Mother Earth, is spoken of as 'walking the Red Road'. For this reason, despite the pejorative use of the term 'redskin' by whites, many Native Americans refer to themselves as 'red'. The messenger of the north is the bald eagle.

East

The east is a solar power, because it is where the sun rises. It brings wisdom and enlightenment (en-lighten-ment), and it is associated with birth and beginnings. The planet Venus, as the Morning Star, is closely associated with the sun and with wisdom, and Lakota people are sometimes buried in Morning Star quilts, since death is seen as birth into another world. The east is the home of the Elk People. The colour of the east is yellow; its messenger is the brown eagle.

South

Lakotas say that someone who has died has 'gone south', because this is the place of death and the spirit world. Thus, south is 'the direction in which we always face'. At the same time, life starts in the south and it is a source of warmth and happiness, and home to the Animal People. Its colour is white; its messenger is the white crane.

Above

Although Native Americans think of the Great Spirit (*Wakan Tanka* in Lakota) as being omnipresent, he is symbolically regarded as being above, and so they raise the sacred pipe to the heavens after praying with it to the four compass points. The Red Road leads to the Great Spirit. He is called Grandfather (in Tunkashila Lakota), rather than Father. His colour is sky-blue.

Below

Below is the realm of Mother Earth, watched over by the Great Spirit. We should pray to her because our bodies come directly from her and we are nourished by her. Her colour, naturally, is green.

The directional associations of other tribes are broadly similar, though they differ in detail – for example, in the colours and sacred beings ascribed. The Navajo have four sacred mountains at the four compass points. In ceremonies, and on their Great Seal, these are depicted in their respective colours: white in the east for White Shell Woman; blue in the south for Turquoise Woman; yellow in the west for Abalone Woman; and black in the north for Jet Black Woman. The Hopi colours, on the other hand, are: yellow in the west, blue in the south, red in the east and white in the north. Those for the Micmac of Canada are: yellow in the west, white in the south, red in the east and black in the north.

The directions within

Native Americans see the directions both as external and inner forces. We have all six within us, and at the same time each individual is at their centre, a focus of cosmic energy. This is highlighted when we place the directions – associated collectively with human life on earth – within the circle of spirit. This forms the mandala of the medicine wheel. The circle is also the path of the sun, and so the wheel is often shown with arms trailing out as if the burning disc of the sun were trailing tongues of fire after it in the colours of the directions (see illustration opposite). This also forms the ancient, multicultural but much-abused symbol of the swastika. Shown with arms trailing as if the four spokes were turning clockwise, it represents the sun. Shown the other way round it represents the turning of the earth in relation to the sun. In Native American perception, the sun turns one way and humans create cosmic balance by turning the other way.

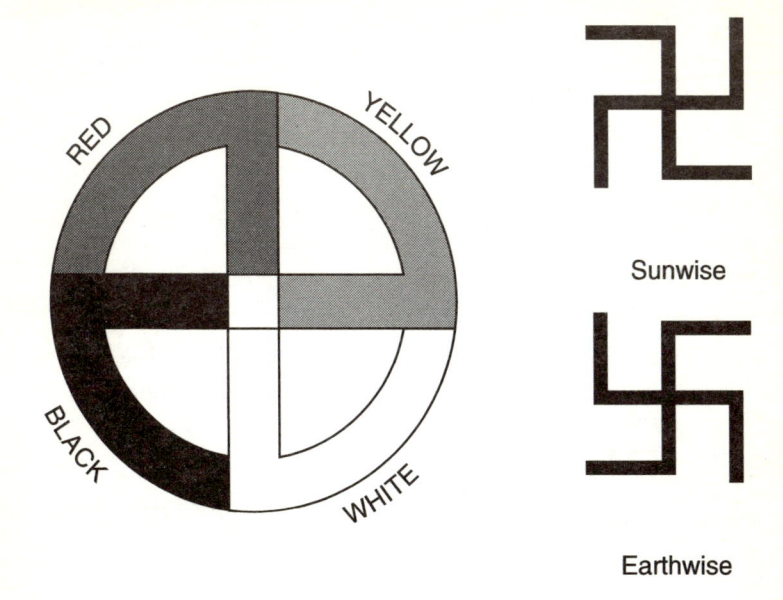

Medicine Wheel and Swastikas

Sacred sites

Native Americans regard the entire earth as holy, an attitude diametrically opposed to that of the invading whites, for whom the land was a commodity to be bought, sold and exploited. At the same time, each tribe felt a deep affinity with the area in which it had lived for centuries. They had no complaints about their homeland, only gratitude and affection, as expressed by Arapooish, a Crow:

> *The Crow country is a good country. The [Creator] put it exactly in the right place; while you are in it you fare well; whenever you are out of it, whichever way you travel, you fare worse. ... The Crow country is exactly in the right place. It has snowy mountains and sunny plains; all kinds of climates and good things for every season. When the summer heats scorch the prairies, you can draw up under the mountains, where the air is sweet and cool, the grasses fresh, and the bright streams come tumbling out of the snowbanks. There you you can hunt the elk, the deer, and the*

antelope, when their skins are fit for dressing; there you will find plenty of white bear and mountain sheep. ...The Crow country is exactly in the right place.[1]

Geronimo, the heroic Apache leader, voiced a similar view – though one now touched by bitterness – when exiled from his homeland:

For each tribe of men Usen created He also made a home. In the land for any particular tribe He placed whatever would be best for the welfare of that tribe.

When Usen created the Apaches He also gave them their homes in the West. He gave them such grain, fruits, and game as they needed to eat. ...He gave them a pleasant climate, and all they needed for clothing and shelter was at hand.

Thus it was in the beginning: the Apaches and their homes each created for the other by Usen himself. When they are taken from these homes they sicken and die.[2]

On a more localized level, all tribes had – and still have – particular sites of special religious importance to them, especially hills, mountains or springs. The peak of Bear Butte in South Dakota, sacred to the Lakota and the Cheyenne, commands an awe-inspiring view of the Plains stretching out into the distant haze to the north and east, and to the dark green of the Black Hills to the south. The path to the summit is lined with scraps of coloured cloth and tobacco prayer 'flags', the colours corresponding to the directions and to the particular kind of help that an individual seeks. Similar ceremonial ribbons are tied to pine trees on top of Harney Peak, the highest and most sacred peak in the Black Hills, on which Lakota medicine man Black Elk once prayed to the Six Powers of the World, and was answered with rain by the Thunder Beings.

The Navajo still inhabit the land between their four holy mountains: Blanca Peak, Colorado; Mount Taylor, New Mexico; the San Francisco Peaks, Arizona; and Hesperus Peak, Colorado. They believe that they have been placed here by the Creator and given the responsibility to live there and care for this land. Their religious ceremonies must be performed at specific sites in this land. Their healing ceremonies must be performed using sand paintings and herbs from freshly gathered local plants and minerals. The medicine man must walk to where the herb grows, tell it the patient's name, and make it offerings of corn pollen, songs and prayers.

At the time of writing, thousands of Navajo are threatened with forced relocation. Mae Tso, a Navajo elder, eloquently explains their position:

> *All of our sacred songs and prayers are here within our four scared mountains. The teachings of our ancestors are here in our songs and prayers. These songs and prayers are part of the ceremonies, they are our teaching and our way of life. This is our religion. This is what connects us to the land. Here, we have always made our offerings to the spiritual beings. Here we are known by the spiritual beings. If we are relocated to the new lands, we would not be known, we could not do our ceremonies. This is our religion, our way of life. If you cut out a person's heart and take it away, the person would die. Our Creator placed us here on this land, we are part of Mother Earth's heart. If you take us away to another land, we will not survive.*[3]

Betty Tso, another Navajo, echoes the Lakota's invocation of all nature, 'All our relatives,' in her words:

> *We the five-fingered beings are related to the four-legged, the winged beings, the spiritual beings, Father Sky, Mother Earth, and nature. We are all relatives. We cannot leave our relatives behind.*[4]

Earth and stars

Most Native American tribes watched the stars and solstices, as well as the phases of the moon, using them for agricultural and ritual purposes. The Zuni used the Plough (Big Dipper) to time planting. The Hopi used the appearance of Orion and the Pleiades through the roof entrances of their ceremonial buildings to time their rituals at night. Archaeology reveals that tribes used the movement of the sunrise north in spring and south in autumn to track the year. The Mescalero Apaches still observe the solstices.

Some sites show sophisticated attempts to relate earth to the movements of the sun, moon and stars. One example is the Big Horn Medicine Wheel, Wyoming. This is 30 metres (100 feet) across, and centres on a cairn 4 metres (13 feet) across. It has 28 'spokes' of small stones and an outer circle of small stones, with six larger cairns positioned along it. Archaeo-astronomer John Eddy found that Big Horn included alignments with the summer solstice dawn and sunset, as well as with the rising of the stars Aldebaran, Rigel and Sirius.

A different kind of relationship is found in the star lore of the Lakota. This relates key sites in the Black Hills to the annual cycle of stars' positions in relation to the sun as it progresses eastwards in relation to the earth. The Lakota identify a number of constellations. These include the Plough (Big Dipper) and the Pleiades, but others are quite different from those of European astronomy and astrology. (See opposite.)

According to living Lakota elders, there exist, or at least recently existed, two very old buffalo hide maps: one of the Black Hills showing rivers, valleys, rock features and mountains, the other showing constellations that correspond to them, bearing out the esoteric adage, 'as above, so below'. One Lakota elder, Stanley Looking Horse, said of the maps: 'They are the same, because what is on the earth is in the stars, and what is in the stars is on the earth.'[5] Amos Bad Heart's map of the Black Hills is shown on page 22. Harney Peak, corresponding to the Pleiades, is shown above Buffalo Gap.

To the Lakota, the stars are the breath of Wakan Tanka, the Great Spirit. It is natural that they should reflect life on earth, as we are spiritual beings passing through a phase of material embodiment, as Mother Earth is married to Father Sky. The constellations reflected in the Black Hills also play a part in Lakota myth. Harney Peak, mentioned above, features in a tale involving a Lakota culture hero, Fallen Star. In this tale, a band is camped near Harney Peak. Each day a red eagle carries off a girl to the mountain peak. The band pray to Fallen Star, and after seven days he comes and shoots the eagle, and then places the girls in the sky as the Pleiades (in Lakota the *Wicincala Sakowin* – Seven Little Girls.

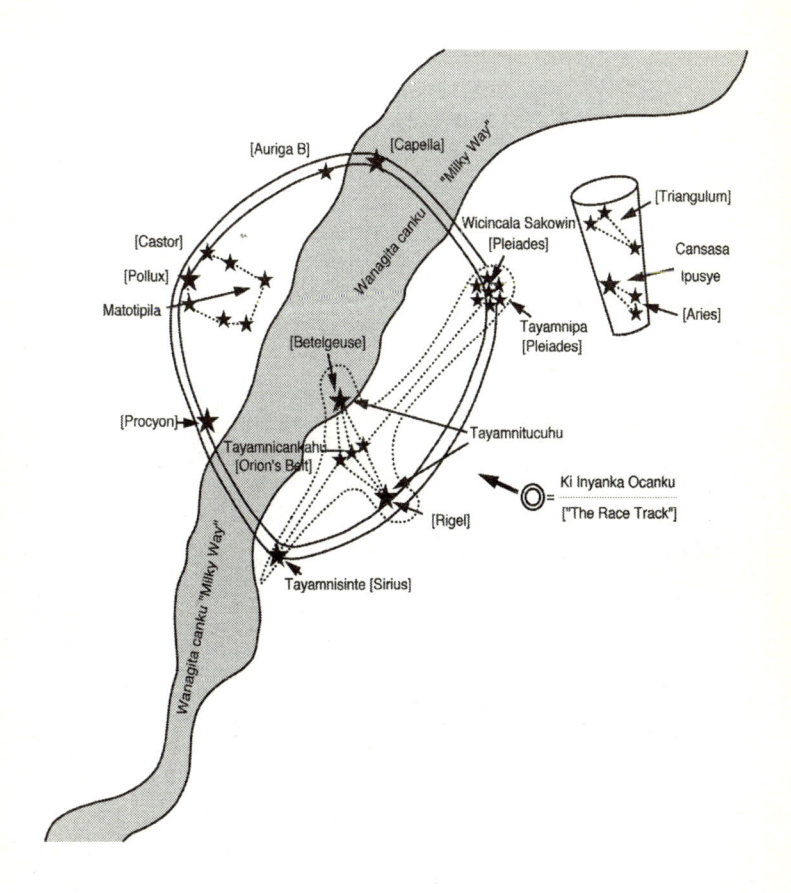

Our place on earth 21

[1] Cansasa Ipusye - Dried Willow;

[2] Wicincala Sakowin - Seven Little Girls;

[3] Tayamni [the group] - An Animal;

[4] Ki Inyanka Ocanku - The Race Track;

[5] Mato Tipila - The Bear's Lodge.

Lakota constellations on ecliptic (west to east)

22 Timeless Wisdom of the Native Americans

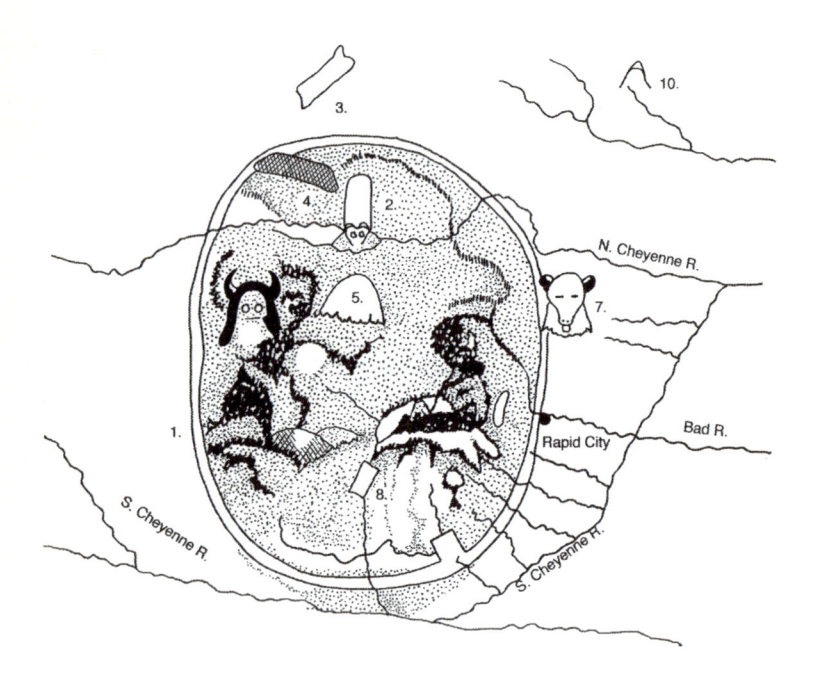

1. Ki Iyanka Ocanku [Race Track]
2. Mato tipi paha [Bear Lodge Butte]
3. Paha zizpela [Slim Buttes]
4. Paha sapa [Black Butte]
5. He sla [Old Baldy]
6. Hinhan kaga paha [Ghost Butte]
7. Mato paha [Bear Butte]
8. Mnikata [Hot Springs]
9. Pte tali yapa [Buffalo Gap]
10. Wakinyan Paha [Thunder Butte]

Amos Bad Heart's map of the Black Hills

Another story describes a race run by the animals to decide the fate of the 'two-leggeds'. This is said to take place around the red clay valley encircling the Black Hills, corresponding to the 'Race Track' constellation.

The constellations also relate to Lakota ritual. The Plough (Big Dipper) is like a wooden spoon carrying the live coal, representing the sun, to light the scared pipe in the Dried Willow constellation. Dried Willow is the constellation of spring, and dried willow itself is what would be smoked in the ritual pipe.

Above all, the Lakota's wanderings over their homeland traced a symbolic path through the constellations. Each spring a group would travel north through the Black Hills, synchronizing their movements and ceremonies with the passage of the sun through the constellations. They believed that the same ceremonies were being performed simultaneously in the spirit world. Their journey was a means of harmonizing the two worlds and drawing down spirit power into this world. They would also be following the buffalo, which is associated with the sun. Thus when Chief Red Cloud in his abdication speech (1903) spoke of the Lakota's need for freedom to roam, he was talking about a spiritual need:

> *We told [the commissioners] that the supernatural power Taku Wakan, had given to the Lakotas the buffalo for food and clothing. We told them that where the buffalo ranged, that was our country. We told them that the country of the buffalo was the country of the Lakotas. We told them that the buffalo must have their country and the Lakotas must have the buffalo.*[6]

Application

We can enrich our lives by becoming aware of the directions. Use a compass to establish where they are, and place objects in a room to represent the elements most commonly associated with them: east – fire (perhaps a candle); south – air (something light that blows in the air); west – water (a cup of water); north – earth (a stone). Alternatively use colours. Sitting at their centre, face each in turn and either contemplate what they represent, or honour them by addressing them, naming their powers and associations, and asking for their help.

Keep track of the sun's path each day, and of the gradual shift of sunrise and sunset north as the summer solstice approaches, and south as the winter solstice approaches. You can also observe the nightly passage of the stars, especially the Pleiades and Orion's belt, and of course the phases of the moon.

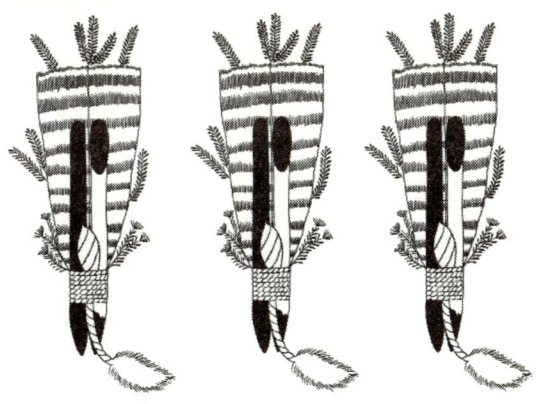

Chapter 4
The spirit world and nature

> *We are all related*
> [Native American saying]

Europeans have for centuries seen a clear-cut distinction between spirit and matter. God is remote from our world. A Lakota joke comments on this:

> *A Lakota has an audience with the Pope. The Pope breaks off to speak on the phone. 'That was God, on the hotline,' he says. 'You can give Him a call – 10 dollars a minute.' The Lakota politely declines. Next year the Pope visits the Lakota's home. 'I've got a hotline, too,' says the Lakota. The Pope uses it to talk to God for half an hour. 'How much will that be?' he asks, reaching for his purse. 'No charge,' says the Lakota: 'Local call!'*

To Native Americans, the spirit world is all around us. All living things, and even rocks and stones, have a spirit. There are also spirits of the dead, as well as a host of others, helpful, harmful, or plain fickle. Some Pacific tribes feared the Cannibal Spirit, or the Bird Spirit, known as Crooked Beak of Heaven, who had to be placated or warded off by dances, songs and rituals. Many Native Americans, however, say that no spirit is evil, and that even the apparently mischievous ones are part of the Great Spirit.

Elders speak of spirits in a respectful but matter-of-fact way, often seeing them as glowing or flickering lights. It may be that those of us who are less aware experience them as changes in our mood. Although many Native Americans see or sense spirits, this happens most often during rituals.

Lakota medicine man Lame Deer gives us a clear idea of how a spirit might manifest, and of the sensitivity of the spirits. A friend had dreamed that he would be cured of a sickness if he lay down beneath the central pole of the Sundance ceremony, but that no one should come near him:

As he was stretched out on the ground, believe it or not, in a few minutes there was somebody in the earth, about 20 feet beneath the surface, walking around there, roaming. Pete could hear him, see him, feel him. There was somebody down there and pretty soon he was coming up, breaking through the earth and rock, hitting his round belly, stretching out his arms, looking at Pete. He was coming to doctor him.

And just at this moment one of the dance leaders took it into his head to show off before the tourists and cameras, waving his eagle fan above Pete, pretending to do a medicine ceremony, wanting to give the spectators their moneys worth. Pete had told everybody to keep away from him, but maybe this man forgot, and that being beneath the earth went away, backed down. It didn't like all the tourist stuff. Pete was so sad he could have cried.[1]

Archetypes

The being described above seems to be an earth spirit. Other spirits can be seen as archetypal forces. In particular there are the spirits of the Six Directions (see page 14), often called on in ritual. Animal spirits are extremely important, again as archetypes. The individual animal or plant has a spirit, but this is part of the greater spirit of its species. The individual is a manifestation of the presiding archetype, which in turn is a manifestation of the Great Spirit.

Certain animal spirits are especially important. For example, to the Plains tribes the Buffalo spirit is very powerful. To the Lakota this is Tatanka (*ta*, 'beast'; *tanka* 'great'). He rules fertility, virtue, industry and family life, and he guards pregnant women. A sense of dynamic dualism is conveyed by the fact that Tatanka is in continual conflict with Mica – Coyote. This very widespread figure is the patron of theft, malevolence and cleverness – and in many myths he is the creator or champion of mankind. In myths of the Papago and Pima peoples of the South-West, Coyote helps to create the earth. Similar in some ways, but generally more malevolent, is Iktome – Spider.

The Bear is the spirit of love, hate, courage, wounds and many medicines. Other rulerships include: Wolf – hunting and war; Dog – friendship and cunning; Male Elk – sexual relationships; Beaver – hard work and fidelity; Eagle – councils and battles.

Some Native American individuals feel a particular affinity with one species, which they may call on for help. They may also avoid eating that animal. This is similar to the attitude of the ancient Celts, though for the Native American there is generally no specific taboo equivalent to the Celtic *geasa* – through which a man might be doomed by killing or eating a certain animal. In some cases whole tribes or clans within tribes might identify with an animal totem and call upon its spirit in ceremony. Among the Hopi, for example, there are Badger, Bear, Snake and Parrot clans. The Tlinglit of Alaska have Bear, Eagle, Wolf and Raven clans.

For the Hopis, the spirits, or Kachinas, are the inner, spiritual elements of external, physical life forms. They can be spirits of minerals, animals, plants, birds or other planets, but there are also Kachinas who are the spirits of especially pure, virtuous humans who have been allowed to go straight to the next universe rather than having to progress through all the worlds of this one. They have opted to return to earth to aid in humanity's spiritual evolution. In this they are rather like the Boddhisattvas of Tibetan Buddhism, who choose to defer Nirvana in order to reincarnate on earth to help others gain enlightenment.

Respect for nature

In the European Christian world, nature has for centuries been something to be tamed and civilized. The Native American, however, perceives the entire natural world as being animated by spirit. Therefore the environment is to be respected and protected. Many nomadic hunter-gatherer tribes of the Plains even objected to farming, feeling that Mother Earth provided for them adequately, and that it would be sacrilege to rake her body with iron tools and plant crops. Others farmed, but did so in a way that was in harmony with nature, blessing the land and making minimal impact on its form.

These people, living close to the land, also saw themselves as being related to all its occupants. When modern Native Americans say, in their different languages, 'All my relatives', this is what they mean – not just human relatives, but all life. Moreover, they feel that all life is interdependent, each species supporting the others in a delicate balance. In the modern world we are finding out that this is true, and that we cannot eliminate a species, or alter the environment, without a chain of consequences.

When Plains tribes went on a buffalo hunt they would first perform rituals to gain the Buffalo Spirit's approval. They would speak respectfully to the animal before killing it, and thank its spirit afterwards for surrendering its body. Moreover, every part of the animal would be used. Even a bull's scrotum found a use – as a cooking pot.

While Nootka tribesmen of the north Pacific coast were killing a whale, they performed rituals to thank it, and while towing it ashore they would promise to honour its spirit. The chief's wife would stay in bed during the hunt, magically tranquillizing the whale. When it came to shore she would welcome it with fresh water and eagle down. The Koyukon tribe of Alaska hunted moose, but if they found a starving moose trapped in snow they would feed it every day until it was strong enough to free itself.

Native American use of the land and its creatures was respectful and sustainable. The white settlers, on the other hand, regarded natural resources as there to be exploited while they lasted. They slaughtered the buffalo in thousands – partly to starve out the Plains tribes. They later turned Oklahoma into a dust bowl. Compare the Native American approach, too, with trophy-hunting, and with modern farming techniques which poison the land and rivers, destroy habitats, and kill whole ecosystems.

For Native Americans, plants, too, had spirits. Interestingly this would be very specific to species. Thus the Micmac have no word for 'tree' – only for individual species of tree. Plant names are mostly based on their properties, helpful or otherwise. For example a Micmac/Cree word for one forest plant, *pipisissiwa*, translates as 'it breaks up' – derived from an older word meaning 'it breaks up kidney stones'.[2]

Animal names, too, reflect the Native American's close observation. For example in many tribal languages the word for rabbit translates as 'his ears are close together'. The Micmac for squirrel translates as 'he comes down head first'.

Time and timelessness

Traditional Native Americans have a sense of time that is quite different from that of non-holistic, industrialized societies but similar to that of the Australian Aborigines and other earth-linked peoples. In the Micmac language, for example, there is no word for time. The concept of time exists, but only in the sense of things happening. Duration of time is measured by how long a task might take. Time of year is expressed in terms of what happens then, usually linked to the moon, giving us 'Leaf Turn Moon', 'Starvation Moon', 'Fish Nesting Moon' and 'Cranberry Moon'. The Lakota speak of the time around August as 'when the cherries turn black'. The Micmac New Year's Day is 'the day of the new moon when the creek freezes'.

Elders say that even these terms were not fixed before the coming of the white man. Rather, a time of year could be named in conversation by any one of a number of events that took place at that time, depending on what was poetically appropriate.

On the grand scale, there are the creation myths, which give events in a sequence, but which are not concerned with dating – 'a very long time ago' is adequate. Coming a little closer to our own time, however, Native Americans do show some concern for recording key tribal or family events, indicating the year and sometimes the season in which they occurred. Typically this was done in picture form on a buffalo hide, as in the Lakota 'winter counts', in which each year was repressed by a single event.

Traditional Native Americans measure time, on a day-to-day level, by the sun and stars. If an appointment is necessary, it may be at dawn or dusk, or when the Pleiades are overhead. It might even be 'when the sun hangs over those trees'. More than likely, however, if you try to fix a meeting with an elder, you will simply be told, 'Just come!' If you do, and are told on arrival, 'Oh, he'll be back sometime later,' this is not a personal insult. Rather, it stems from a belief that if a meeting is to happen, it will happen at the right time, when it is meant to happen.

Above all, the Native American lives in the present, not clock-watching, not worrying about the past or future. Patience is a Native American virtue. For the Micmacs it is symbolized by the heron, who waits motionless for as long as it takes for its meal to swim by – then acts fast when it does. The Spider Clan of the Osage tribe took the spider as their totem because of this same virtue. Things take as long as they take. This is part of the secret of Native American crafts. For example, the process of working with porcupine quills can take a hundred hours. They must be soaked, plucked and flattened. The dye must be prepared; then there is the dying itself, the drying, and the careful, painstaking weaving into patterns and shapes, such as medicine wheels. A contemporary Plains woman, Alice New Holy, who produces exquisite quillwork in the traditional style, comments: 'It was something I had to learn. All Indian girls had to learn quillwork. It teaches you how to sit still and do something.'[3]

It is also part of the Native American view that time is circular rather than linear, not just in terms of the sun's daily progress and the season, but in what happens. Opportunities will come around again. If something is meant to happen, it will somehow 'fall together', if not today then tomorrow. We will all meet again one never says 'Goodbye' to a Native American: 'So long' or 'See you around' are preferred, as being less final.

Finally, part and parcel of this world-view is the belief that things are constantly changing. This is like the Buddhist concept of *anicca* (pronounced 'anicha'), or impermanence. Thus the world is vibrant and alive, doing rather than just being. This is expressed in some Native American languages, such as Micmac, by there being very few nouns in general use. A noun implies something static.

Instead these languages use descriptive, and often poetic, verbal phrases. The colour blue is *moos-seh-geesq-chamough* – 'it is being the colour of the sky'; the colour green is *neebuchtamough* – 'it is being the colour of the woods in spring'. A mole is *moolumpgwedjeedj* – 'someone small with four legs digging underground'. One does, however, find nouns in the Micmac creation story, suggesting a universe whose basic components are fixed.

Visitors from the spirit world

Dreams are one means by which the spirit world communicates with us, and we can open ourselves up to this world by considering what our dreams are telling us. A Native American might consult a medicine man for guidance on this. Most Europeans will have to rely on their own intuition, as there is no effective 'guide' to dream interpretation. Perhaps for a people more in touch with the spirit world, or with a more uniform collective unconscious, it was possible to be more prescriptive.

For the Lakota, dreams could be prophetic, or could confer powers or obligations. A man who dreamed of a bear was said to be holy; one who dreamed of the wolf was thought to have the ability to creep up on an enemy; someone who dreamed of the coyote would have to wear a coyote skin to hunt and kill a buffalo, after which he could discard the skin. A white bear dream warned against eating heart or liver. The Menominee tribe of the Great Lakes region believed that anyone whose dream could not be interpreted, or who never dreamed, was out of touch with the spirit world.

A particularly strong obligation fell to any Lakota who dreamed of the Wakinyan – the Thunder Spirits. This person would have to become a *heyoka*. To be a heyoka was an honour – but also a burden! The heyoka would have to do everything back to front: saying yes for no; going half-naked on a freezing day and complaining of the heat; walking backwards; saying the opposite of what he really meant. He would also be obliged to act out his dreams publically, no matter how embarrassing. The heyoka was thus a kind of 'lord of misrule', something like a court jester or Shakespearean Fool, entertaining people and reminding them of the existence of duality and disorder. Even now, someone might vow to become a heyoka for a set period of time to secure the favour of the spirit world – for example, to help a sick relative.

The spirit world might also manifest in visions. Oglala Lakota medicine man Black Elk received his great vision at the age of nine, when he lay in a coma for twelve days. He saw horses coming from all directions of the sky, and was given healing powers by the Grandfathers of the Six Directions (see page 14). He saw the good Red Road of the medicine wheel and the Black Road of destruction, and a soaring vision of world harmony, glimpsed from what he later identified as Harney Peak in the Black Hills:

> *I saw more than I can tell and I understood more than I saw; for I was seeing in a sacred manner the shapes of all things in the spirit, and the shape of all shapes as they must live together like one being. And I saw that the sacred hoop of my people was one of many hoops that made one circle, as wide as daylight and as starlight, and in the centre grew one mighty flowering tree to shelter all the children of one mother and one father. And I saw that it was holy.*[4]

Crying for a vision

A very deliberate way in which the spirits are contacted is the vision quest, in Lakota the *hanblechia*, also known as 'crying for a vision'. This is essential for a young male entering manhood, but it may also be done whenever someone of either sex seeks spiritual guidance or power. The Lakota war leader Crazy Horse is said to have received much of his power from vision quests. The Lakota and Cheyenne were encouraged to take on General Custer at the Little Big Horn in 1876 by a vision given to Sitting Bull in which he saw 'many white soldiers falling backwards into camp'.

It is important for the seeker to secure the help of a medicine man. He does this formally, offering him a pipe. The medicine man helps the seeker to prepare himself by taking part in the sweatlodge ceremony (see page 61). Then the seeker must sit or stand in a narrow, grave-like pit on a remote hilltop, wearing only a buffalo robe or blanket, for several days and nights. A woman seeker will normally go to somewhere less remote, perhaps staying within the sweatlodge. Four flags with tobacco ties – little bundles of tobacco – are positioned as offerings at the corners of the pit for the four earthly directions. The seeker may take a gourd containing small pieces of flesh which a female relative has cut from her arms to encourage him, or he may sacrifice small pieces of his own flesh. Sitting Bull cut a hundred pieces from each of his arms when seeking his vision before Little Big Horn.

The seeker remains praying fervently for a vision, and occasionally smoking a pipe of red willow bark tobacco, for as long as four days and nights, or as long as it takes for the vision to unfold. During this time the seeker goes without food or water, which weakens the normal logical processes, making a vision more easily attainable.

In the quest described by Black Elk in *The Sacred Pipe,* the vision pit is replaced by a sacred space marked by poles at the four earthly directions. The seeker must move from one pole to another, always going via a central pole (perhaps symbolizing a continual centring within oneself), praying: 'Wakan Tanka, pity me that my people may live.' Black Elk says that the seeker should pay close attention to any creatures that visit, such as ants, birds or squirrels, as the spirit may convey its messages through them as much as through an inner vision.

Many Native Americans have a spirit name which is given to them by a medicine man after their first vision quest, based either on their vision or on the medicine man's vision. It is thought that this is their 'true name', without which they will not be known in the spirit world. Crazy Horse received his name from a vision of a prancing horse.

There are many variations on the type of vision quest described above. For example, Papago and Pima boys have to run until they fall down exhausted, and then pray for an animal spirit guide. What most have in common is solitary withdrawal, abstinence, and contemplation or prayer.

Divination

Most cultures have some traditional form of divination (*divination*: communication with the divine), used to understand a situation or to predict the future. Christianity has tended to regard prophecy as a challenge to the will of God. In some cultures there are highly developed systems of divination; the *I Ching* is a classic example. There are few, if any, systems of this sort native to North America. Anything purporting to be 'Native American astrology', or any Tarot-like system based on 'medicine cards', is synthetic – even if it does stem from a native tradition.

Traditional Native American divination is often practised by interpretation of dreams or visions, usually by a medicine man or woman. This gifted person might also practise a variety of techniques that could be seen as ways of accessing his or her own inner vision. A Huron diviner might apply to a familiar spirit, or gaze into a bowl of water, or into fire. These methods might help to find lost objects, predict the future, or cure the sick. A Navajo diviner might practise the art of 'hand-trembling', in which after purification by washing with yucca root (a form of natural soap), he would perform a ceremony beseeching the Gila Monster (a lizard) to reveal answers to questions. He would then interpret the subsequent trembling of his own hand.

Medicine men and women would also 'read' the language of nature, such as the flight of birds, echoing techniques practised by many peoples – including the Celts. A Jungian analyst would say this worked by allowing open-minded individuals to tap into their own unconscious knowledge, since we tend to notice only those natural phenomena that are relevant to our situation or which give us correct answers. A Native American would say that nature spoke to the person prepared to listen and skilled in understanding.

The same interpretation could be given to any ready-made formula. For example, Jamie Sams,[5] a member of the Seneca tribe, writes that the markings on stones can teach us about our natural potential:

Straight vertical line	Spirit power to overcome material challenges
Crossed arrows pointing up	Power of mutual friendship and respect
Square	Stability; organizational ability
Diamond	Life, unity, equality, freedom from fear; the protection of the Four Winds

In Sams' terms, the stone speaks; in Jungian terms, the stone is a vehicle enabling us to contact our inner knowledge. Perhaps the difference is only one of perspective – though it has to be said that in many ways the Native American view of a living, speaking world is more appealing.

Application

A real vision quest requires personal guidance. However, it is possible to gain some of the benefits of being in nature without distractions, and of solitude and fasting. Those unaccustomed to fasting should probably not try to go without water, or to fast for longer than a day or so. Cut yourself off from people, distractions and comforts as much as possible, so that you rely on inner resources and on the spirit world. It is also essential to come back into everyday life gently, eating lightly at first and allowing yourself time to adjust and assimilate insights.

Even without fasting, if we go into nature alone, deliberately open to messages about our lives, or asking a question, we may be given answers. If you normally walk through the countryside without stopping, perhaps chatting with a friend, you may be surprised by what you receive when you stay quietly in one place, even for a short time, attentive to nature.

Whether in nature, or at home, try to get by without a watch. The sky should give you all the indication of time you need.

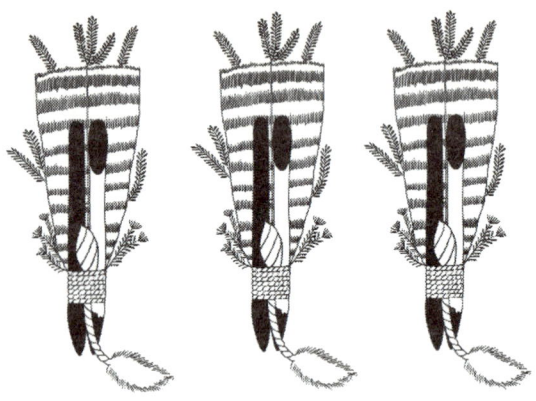

Chapter 5
Symbolism and the arts

The white man sees so little he must see with only one eye.

[Lakota]

Lame Deer has the following to say about the difference between European and Native American attitudes to symbolism:

> *We see a lot that you no longer notice. You could notice if you wanted to, but you are usually too busy. We Indians live in a world of symbols and images where the spiritual and the commonplace are one. To you symbols are just words, spoken or written in a book. To us they are part of nature, part of ourselves – the earth, the sun, the wind and the rain, stones, trees, animals, even little insects like ants and grasshoppers. We try to understand them not with the head but with the heart, and we need no more than a hint to give us the meaning.*
>
> *What to you seems commonplace, to us appears wondrous through symbolism. This is funny, because we don't even have a word for symbolism, yet we are all wrapped up in it. You have the word, but that is all.*[1]

Sacred architecture

Lame Deer's words point to a fundamental difference between European and Native American thinking. The average European lives in a world that has no inherent meaning, that has nothing to say. A European house reflects only its owner's material expectations and certain economic factors. Only in dreams might it become a symbol of something else, such as the psyche. The Native American, on the other hand, thinks in a more poetic, right-brain way. Thus, a traditional Native American home is full of a symbolism that has evolved in a way that naturally reflects the cosmos in miniature.

The Navajo's family home, the *hogan*, reflects their homeland. The four posts of the hogan echo the four sacred mountains, which in turn stand for the four earthly directions and the four elements from which, philosophically speaking, everything on earth is made. The hogan is made, according to instructions contained in the Navajo creation story, of logs, bark and earth. The packed earth floor represents Mother Earth, the dome-shaped roof, Father Sky. The hogan is sanctified by the ceremonies that take place in it.

The traditional buffalo hide tipi (later made of canvas) of the Plains peoples similarly reflects the cosmos. The tipi is circular, embodying the circle of spirit, and it extends to a point where its poles cross. This is the point at which stellar or spirit power crosses over into the material world. The tipi thus funnels down the power of spirit. Put another way, it represents a prayer being answered. The poles create a triangle reflecting the lower triangle of hides: as above, so below.

The way in which the tipi reflects the cosmos is shown in the custom whereby the Osage tribe freed the souls of those whom they had slain in battle. The chief would quickly thrust the scalps of the slain on a pole through the hole at the top of the tipi, and then withdraw it. Outside of the tipi, the souls were thought to have left the cosmos, or at least this world, and returned to the infinite.

According to Norbert Running,[2] of the Rosebud Sioux Reservation, when a tipi is built the first three poles erected are a star. The next seven represent the directions (including 'Within'). These first ten are the laws of the world. Another two poles are added outside, the 'ears' to control the tipi's air flow. The tipi can then breathe, or communicate with spirit above. The total of 12 may symbolize twelve months – though some bands used 16 poles, or even more. Black Elk speaks of 28, with the 28th pole supporting all the others and therefore representing Wakan Tanka. The tipi would traditionally be protected by painted scenes or figures representing significant dreams or visions of its inhabitants.

Traditionally the tipi faced east, to honour the rising sun. Men normally sat in the north of the tipi, and women in the west. The single circle of one family's tipi was within the larger circle of the camp, and when the whole tribe met annually, the camp circles of each band were within the all-encompassing circle of the tribe.

The Hopi ceremonial chamber, the *kiva*, also embodies its own symbolism. It is built partially underground, into the womb of Mother Earth, with the east–west path of the sun running along its length. Sometimes it is widened at one end, so that its form resembles the traditional Hopi hairstyle with its thick 'bangs' at the side. Inside, the eastern half of the kiva is raised slightly above the western half. During initiation ceremonies the priests sit barefoot in the lower half, showing their humility. In the centre is a sunken fire pit, symbolizing the beginnings of life in the First World. Next to it is a small hole in the ground, the *sipápuni*, derived from the Hopi words for 'navel' and 'path from'. Thus it represents humanity's umbilical attachment to Mother Earth, and the emergence from the previous world.

The raised level on which the altar stands represents the Second World. The Third World (the one previous to this) is represented by a further level, from which a ladder leads up to the entrance, which is in the roof. This ladder represents the road up which humanity climbed in their emergence into the present world.

Sacred art

In many Native American languages there are no words for religion, symbolism, music or art. This is because these things are integrated into life. A Native American making a functional object would find it natural to make it beautiful as well, either by its design, or by decorating it. Numerous examples are displayed in museums as works of art. However, there is no traditional

Native American 'art for art's sake'; there are beautiful objects which are materially functional – clothes, weapons, cradleboards, pots, baskets. There are also objects that are ritually functional, such as the Seneca and Iroquois 'false face' masks used in healing, or that have a magical function by proclaiming the spirit guardians of their owners, as with the huge totem poles outside houses on the Pacific seaboard.

These items do have an element of pure decoration – a delight in form and colour – but this merges with an underlying awareness of symbolism, a natural tendency to mirror the cosmos. One example of this is in a typical design on the rawhide *parfleche* (from the French, 'deflect arrows'), a kind of satchel traditionally used by the Cheyenne and Lakota to carry small goods (see page 40). The parfleche is not a religious artefact, and its decoration on one level springs from a natural desire to make an everyday object pleasing to the eye. Yet at the same time, it contains religious symbolism.

In this example, the upper and lower pointed cones represent Grandfather Sky and Grandmother Earth meeting in sacred talk. Seen another way, Grandmother Earth sends up a prayer to which Grandfather Sky responds. The Lakota word for prayer is *wacekiya*, which also means 'talking with relatives'. This relates to the Lakota invocation *Mitakuye oyasin* – 'all my relatives'. The two triangles, whose points meet the points of Grandfather Sky and Grandmother Earth at the centre of the parfleche, are the two sacred mountains. The central point is the fire in the tipi, and the individual human heart. The four converging points are also the directions, in which all the spiritual 'relatives' live.

Moving outwards from the centre, the shapes around the triangles are wings, taking prayer to heaven. The border pattern could be seen as mountains – perhaps the sacred Black Hills, or the alternation of opposites.

This parfleche is thus a mandala, a sacred pattern by which the individual can become centred, or can enter the spirit world. The Navajo use this concept in a dynamic way in their healing rituals, in which a patient sits at the centre of a mandala made with different types of coloured sand. This portrays, in physical form,

Lakota parfleche

the idea that the individual is the centre of the universe, and must be in tune with it to be healthy.

The Hopi make particularly complex use of ceremonial artefacts. For example, a *páho* (prayer feather) is used in all ceremonies – see the illustration below that shows the male and female páho. This is made of two red willow sticks of about 20 centimeters (8 inches) long. Both may be painted blue – for sky, water and spirituality – or the 'female' may be blue and the 'male' black. The female stick has a facet cut into the top and painted brown, for Mother Earth. A small cornhusk sack tied to the base of the sticks represents the spiritual body. It contains cornmeal (symbolizing the physical body), corn pollen (fertility), and honey (the Creator's love). The sticks are tied together because the Creator is both male and female, and because both sexes combine to create new life. The cotton cord which binds them is the life cord, an umbilical cord channeling the energy of the sun. A downy eagle feather tied to it represents the breath of life. A turkey feather is tied to the back of the sticks, for the mystery of creation, and herbs are added which represent summer and healing.

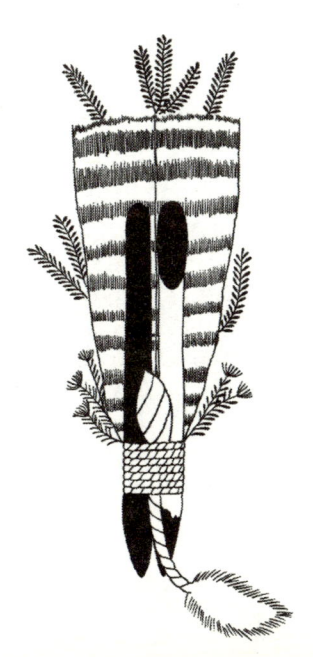

Male and female páho

Another way in which symbolism might be used is in pictorally telling a story. Some Lakota symbols are shown below.

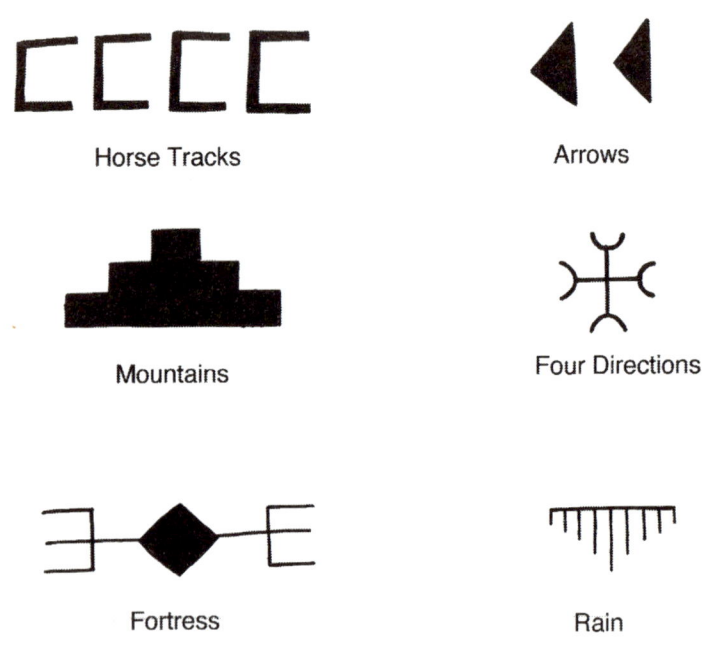

Horse Tracks	Arrows
Mountains	Four Directions
Fortress	Rain

Lakota symbols

Power or superstition?

There is no naturalistic tradition in Native American art, and no 'art for art's sake'. A story told by George Catlin, a portrait painter who travelled across North America in the early nineteenth century, illustrates what happened on one occasion when the Lakota first encountered naturalistic portraits. It also points to the power that traditional Native American peoples ascribed to artistic representations. Catlin had painted several chiefs, and those Lakotas who saw the portraits were awed by the way in which the likenesses seemed to make living doubles of their subjects. He describes what took place when he was painting a distinguished warrior, Mah-to-chee-ga (Little Bear):

> *While I was painting, and had the portrait pretty well advanced, one of the secondary chiefs, by the name of Shon-ka (the Dog), and whose portrait I had painted some days before, rather a surly-looking fellow, and somewhat sarcastic, crept round behind me, and for a while overlooked the operation of my brush, having a full view of the portrait. Being an evilly-disposed man, disliked by most of his fellow-chiefs, and jealous of this rising warrior, he addressed to him this insulting remark – 'I see that you are but half a man.'*
>
> *'Who says that?' said Mah-to-chee-ga, in a low tone of voice, and without the change of a muscle or the direction of his eye.*
>
> *'Shon-ka says it,' replied the Dog.*
>
> *'Let Shon-ka prove it,' replied Mah-to-chee-ga.*
>
> *'Shon-ka proves it in this way; the white medicine man knows that one half of your face is good for nothing, as he has left it out in the picture.'*
>
> *Mah-to-chee-ga replied, 'If I am but half a man, I am man enough for Shon-ka in any way he pleases to try it.'[3]*

Catlin relates how this exchange became heated, leading to Shon-ka fetching his rifle and shooting Mah-to-chee-ga dead, in the process blowing away the half of Mah-to-chee-ga's face that was left out of the portrait. People started to blame Catlin, and even when the chiefs were satisfied of his innocence, the medicine man still insisted that Catlin's 'medicine' was evidently such that he knew that one half of Mah-to-chee-ga's face was no good, and that his revealing this fact had caused the tragedy.

Although there is an element of superstition at work here, the incident may demonstrate a kind of prophecy, and obviously did so to the right-brain thinking of Catlin's accusers, to whom cause and effect do not seem to follow the same one-way chronology that they do in European thinking. At the least, it seems that an artistic representation or symbol has the power to harness the imagination of the beholder.

Application

Symbolic objects can powerfully affect our imagination, and therefore our lives. Make a 'medicine bundle' of objects representing one of the following:

- Your most important beliefs
- Your personal strengths
- The spirit powers of the natural world

You might wish to include something for each of the Six Directions, or for the most important people in your life. Natural objects such as stones, feathers or pieces of bark may be helpful. The choice is yours. Wrap your objects in leather or cloth. Use your bundle as a focus for contemplation or as a talisman. Alternatively, if you are artistically inclined, you could paint a parfleche design embodying your own beliefs.

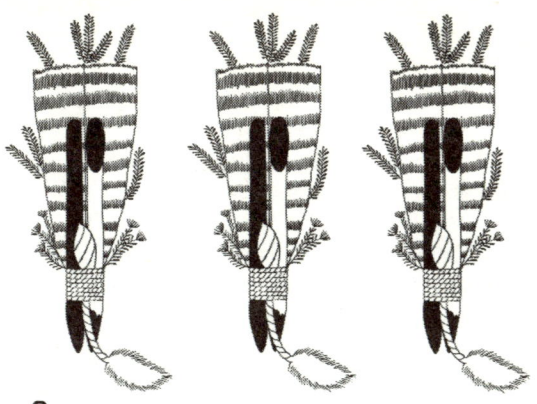

Chapter 6
Gateways

Let us be a spirit,
Let the spirit come from the mouth.
I own this lodge
Through which I pass.

[Midewin initiation song]

Most Native American peoples have a strong sense of life progressing in a predictable sequence, from birth, to puberty, to marriage and childbirth, to death, and either reincarnation or a one-way journey to the spirit world. Thus the individual life follows a path something like that of the seasons. Its key stages are marked by rituals, and there is particular wisdom associated with each of them. The rituals are often regarded as having been given to the tribe by a culture hero, such as White Buffalo Calf Woman for the Lakota, Changing Woman for the Navajo, or Másaw for the Hopi. Thus the rituals are not merely practices that have evolved and been hallowed by time, or that have been devised by a priesthood. Rather, they are sacred instructions that come direct from the spirit world, on a par with Christ's instructions for Holy Communion as followed by Christians.

Birth and childhood

Many Native American peoples believe that children come from either the stars or the sun. They are thought of as especially holy because they have come from the spirit world – an idea also found in the writings of European mystics and poets, from Plato to Blake and Wordsworth. Some attach significance to the soft spot on top of a baby's head where there is a gap in the skull, believing that spirit enters through this place, and that the baby is not fully incarnated until the gap closes up.

The Hopi believe that what happens above ground is mirrored by what happens below. This extends to human life: the spirit of the dead travels, like the sun, beneath the earth and is reborn like the rising sun. Hence the newborn baby is kept in darkness for twenty days, and then carried to the east and held up to the rising sun, the mother saying: 'This is your child.' It may be that this twenty-day period is related to the time the Hopi are supposed to have spent underground in an ant hill before their emergence, but it may also have beneficial effects on the baby, allowing it to adjust gradually to life outside the womb.

Lakota myth tells of two women who wanted to marry stars – perhaps symbolizing spiritual aspiration. They succeed in doing this, and are transported into the stellar spirit world, where they become pregnant by their husbands. The women are warned not to dig wild turnips in their new homeland. However, one of them does, and in so doing she creates a hole in the sky through which she glimpses her old home. She becomes homesick and braids a rope of turnips in order to return – the rope suggesting an umbilical cord, and the woman's homesickness – perhaps representing the way in which the soul is drawn back into incarnation. Unfortunately the rope is too short, and she falls. She is killed, but her baby is born. He is the Lakota culture hero, Fallen Star (see pages 20–23).

In an Arapaho version of the story a girl, Sapana, the most beautiful girl in her village, pursues a porcupine up a cottonwood tree because she wants its quills. As she climbs, the tree stretches higher and higher, and the porcupine stays out of reach. Suddenly she finds herself in a campground in the sky. The porcupine has turned into an ugly old man who takes Sapana for his bride. He sets her to work for him, but warns her not to dig too deep for turnips. One day she digs out a big, deep-rooted turnip, and sees earth through the hole she has made. Homesick like her Lakota counterpart, she saves up strips of buffalo sinew, then ties them into a rope and lowers herself down through the turnip hole. The rope turns out to be too short and, just as her husband is shouting threats from above, a buzzard rescues her. When the buzzard tires, a hawk helps out, and then finally the buzzard delivers Sapana to her village. Her mother is overjoyed to see her, having thought her dead. Again, there are hints of reincarnation, but this time without the birth of Fallen Star.

The Lakota story's 'turnip hole' in the sky is said to be in the centre of the main body of the constellation of the Plough (Big Dipper). According to some Lakota myths, the spirit incarnates through this hole – and returns to the spirit world through it after death. Lakota midwives appeal for help to a deity known as To Win – Blue Woman – who lives near this 'turnip hole'. The Lakota midwife was either called to her vocation through dreams or visions, or was gradually recognized by the community for her skills. She advised the mother-to-be throughout pregnancy as well as supervising the labour. The pregnant woman was not mollycoddled, as it was believed that pregnancy made her stronger. However, she was advised on the importance of a balanced diet according to the Lakota concept of the four meat groups: underwater; underground; on the earth; and above the earth (birds). Vegetables and fruit were to be be eaten only in small quantities.

When the mother first felt the baby inside her there would be a welcoming ceremony, and this is still observed today. The two parents and their families start to talk to the unborn baby, welcoming it and telling it that they are happy that it is coming to them – which must have a positive effect for all concerned.

At the labour, the midwife would help with herbs if necessary, and with prayers and songs. After the birth she would wash her hands ritually and then insert a finger into the baby's mouth to remove any mucus. It was thought that this act might also give the baby some of the midwife's personal character. The midwife would clean the baby, at the same time looking for signs of reincarnation, such as ear lobes already pierced, or scars from the Sundance (see page 67). Twins, thought to be very special even now, are particularly likely to be reincarnated souls come to restore spiritual knowledge.

Particularly interesting is the continuing Lakota custom of keeping the *chekpa* – the umbilical cord. This is thought to prevent the child from becoming restless and nosey – 'always looking for his chekpa'. A boy's cord is sown into a pouch in the shape of a salamander, said to confer adaptability and agility, and to make the boy hard to kill. A girl's cord is sown into a pouch in the shape of a turtle, thought to confer longevity, courage and determination. The pouches are beautifully decorated with beads.

The salamander and turtle are also constellations, and are therefore of the spirit world. The pouches are a means of preserving the child's connection to the spirit world. When the child grows up and is given the pouch, it acts as a reminder of this connection which may give strength at special times, such as when seeking a vision.

A Navajo woman in labour is helped by the Blessingway chant, which recounts the story of Navajo creation (see pages 11–12). Her friends and family might untie the braids of their hair, or even free livestock in order to 'untie' and simplify the birth. The newborn baby is anointed with sacred corn. The baby's first laugh is celebrated, but the child is not formally welcomed into the tribe and introduced to the 'Holy People' until the age of seven – for many tribes the age at which the child is fully incarnated.

The umbilical cord is also important to the Navajo, who bury it near the family home to symbolize the baby's transition from taking its nourishment direct from its mother's womb to a life of being nurtured by Mother Earth. The afterbirth is presented to a young tree, such as a pinon or juniper. Thereafter the tree and the child grow together and are thought to share a lasting spiritual bond. The child's cradleboard is cut from the same tree, and this is offered back to the tree once the child has learned to walk.

Hopi children aged between six and eight are initiated into one of two religious societies: the Powamu for more serious-minded children, and the Kachina for others. The ceremony takes place every four years. It continues on and off for four days, with dancing by adults who take on the roles of *Kachinas* – spirits – and instruction in the form of song. At the climax on the fourth day, each child must step inside a hoop of feathers which is moved up and down four times. Then kachinas pass 'Corn Mothers' up and down the child to promote growth. There follows a final stage that for Europeans raises difficult questions about cultural autonomy and individual rights. In this, all children selected for the Powamu society are flogged with yucca (cactus) whips by two horn-masked whippers of terrifying appearance. They are urged on by a 'Whipper Mother', who also supplies them with fresh whips as they wear out.

Europeans should not condemn this ordeal unthinkingly. It may develop mutual bonds between the children, as well as a sense of belonging. Moreover, within a context of love and concern, perhaps it is more character building than damaging.

Puberty and marriage

These two stages are grouped together because for many tribes, one traditionally follows closely on the heels of the other. Many tribes celebrated a youth's first achievements in the 'manly' pursuits of hunting or warfare; for example, for some north-eastern tribes, when a boy killed his first moose he became eligible to vote and to marry. Spiritual initiations were equally important – for example, the vision quest of the Lakota (see pages 32–33), after which a youth was considered mature enough to marry.

A girl's reaching puberty was traditionally celebrated by many tribes – surely a more healthy approach than the European one of hushing it up or trying to ignore it? A Navajo girl would be sponsored by a woman of another clan, and dressed as a 'White Shell Woman'. There would be a four-day ceremony involving chanting and dancing, ending in marriage. This would traditionally be arranged by the parents, but according to the young couple's preferences.

Black Elk tells how the Lakota puberty rite for girls was received in a vision by a man called Slow Buffalo. In the vision he saw a buffalo cow cleaning its female calf. The first girl to receive this rite was White Buffalo Woman Appears. The rite involves careful honouring of the Six Directions with offerings of tobacco. The medicine man then blows red smoke over the girl. Then he digs a shallow hole, like a buffalo wallow, and makes a cross of tobacco inside it. The hole represents the universe, and the tobacco the earth. He then places blue paint on the tobacco, representing the uniting of sky and earth. A bowl of water with cherries is placed before a specially painted buffalo skull. The girl holds up a sacred bundle of sweetgrass, cherry tree bark and hair from a live buffalo. In a communion with the spirit, she drinks from the bowl, and eats buffalo meat placed in her mouth by the medicine man. Black Elk relates that when White Buffalo Woman Appears emerged from the tipi there was much rejoicing, and people wanted to touch her to share some of her newly acquired holiness.

Among the Hopi it was normal for young people to experiment with *dumaiyas* – love trysts. Once a couple were engaged, the girl would go to live in the boy's family home for three days, during which time she would demonstrate her household skills to the boy's mother. A mock battle would take place outside between the boy's female relatives on his mother's side and father's side, and there would be good natured teasing of the couple. At the end of the three days the couple would pray to the rising sun together and thus become husband and wife.

Hopis and Navajos do not marry within their own clan. The Lakota, like many Native American tribes, are terrified of the slightest hint of incest, so marriage outside of the band is encouraged. For this reason many marriages, traditionally, were made when the entire tribe met for the annual Sundance in the Black Hills. There was an element of parental arrangement; fathers would want their daughters to go to a young man with horses and status. However, there was a tradition called 'He wanted her so much that we gave her to him' whereby a poor but devoted young man could win the bride of his dreams. Otherwise, if he could find a way to arrange it, the couple could elope. After a few days the family would accept the marriage as a *fait accompli* rather than have a dishonoured daughter on their hands. The young man's wooing might be aided by his flute playing, and he might compose a melody which only his sweetheart would recognize, and which would be the signal for their elopement.

Privacy was hard to come by for Lakota lovers. Prospective couples would get to know each other standing wrapped in one blanket outside the tipi. In the Lakota wedding ceremony, too, the couple are wrapped in a single blanket. They also have their wrists bound together with a strip of red cloth, their hands jointly grasping the sacred pipe. Prayers are said, and the pipe is smoked. In a big wedding there would also be presents, drummers, songs and more prayers.

The spirit journey

Native Americans view death in various ways, but all regard it as a gateway to another world, not an end. There is widespread belief in reincarnation, but also in a kind of heaven – dubbed by the white man as 'the Happy Hunting Ground'. Another key point is that there is no concept of hell or purgatory. What happens to the individual after death does not depend on how he or she has lived life on earth – except that in some tribes especially virtuous individuals may be blessed in some way, for example by being spared future reincarnations – as is the case with the Hopi. The Wabanaki of the North-East believe that, through successive reincarnations, individuals progress along the medicine wheel until they are finally pure, when they may choose to return to help the living. Again, this is similar to Hopi belief, as well as to that of Tibetan Buddhism.

To the Lakota, the soul passes through the hole in the sky in the centre of the Plough (Big Dipper). It travels along the Milky Way, the pathway of the dead, either to a happy land, like this one but without hardship (like the Celtic Land of the Blessed), or to reincarnation. All Lakotas accept that some souls are reincarnated. Some think that all are, in a continual alternation between this world and the spirit world. Some say that the soul travels south along the Milky Way to a fork in the path. Here an old woman, Maya Owichapaha ('she who pushes them over the bank') judges souls, allowing the pure to take the right-hand path towards Wakan Tanka, while the rest must take the left-hand path and remain in a conditioned state until they are purified – presumably by further incarnation. In some ways this is similar to the Buddhist belief, according to which, only when the soul is freed from craving and aversion can it attain Nirvana.

Although the Lakota do not see death as a bad thing for the individual, the bereaved do mourn their loved ones keenly. Sometimes they might cut themselves, or at least cut off their hair, to show how they miss the person they have lost. However, there is a strong feeling that life must go on, supported by the family and the tribe. It is still common for relatives to burn the possessions of the deceased, partly so that the spirit's journey will be less hampered by clinging to earthly things, and partly so that the surviving relatives will not be constantly reminded of the deceased and therefore unable to get on with their lives. Similarly, the Yuma tribe of the South-West would burn the deceased's home or, if relatives still lived there, make a new door and smokehole so that the dead could not find their way back in.

A death may also be associated with a 'giveaway', when the immediate family give away some of their most valued possessions. In the past, families would sometimes literally give away the shirts off their backs, both to honour the deceased and as a means of easing their grief by freely relinquishing their hold on the material world from which their loved one had departed.

The Lakota practised a ceremony for the 'keeping' of the soul of the deceased. This is said to have originated with the keeping of a dead child's soul by the parents, and this is the purpose mentioned by Lame Deer.[1] However, Black Elk says that the ceremony came to be used to 'keep' the souls of great leaders first, and then of most good people.[2]

Keeping a soul was a serious undertaking. The keeper had to take a lock of the deceased's hair and purify it with sweetgrass smoke. The lock was then wrapped in buckskin and the bundle put in a special place in the tipi, where it was prayed and smoked over. The keeper had to live a very pure life while keeping the soul, never taking part in battle or hunting, or even using a knife. A woman would be appointed to take special care of the bundle in the tipi, and would prepare food for it which would be kept in a decorated buffalo-hide box until the day that the soul was to be released. On fine days the bundle had to be taken out and hung on a tripod facing south – the direction in which the soul would eventually travel to the spirit land.

The eventual releasing of the soul, usually after a year, would be accompanied by prayers and offerings to the Six Directions, and smoking of the pipe. The bowl of the pipe would first be held over a hot coal on which was burned a sacred herb, so that the smoke from the herb wafted through the pipe and into the air through the stem, which was held towards the heavens. In this way the pipe was first smoked by Wakan Tanka.

Women would bring offerings of food into the tipi, inside which would be a willow staff topped by a face painted on buckskin to represent the soul about to be released. This would stand in the south of the tipi. The face would wear a war bonnet, and a buffalo robe would be draped around the staff. The deceased's possessions would be leaning against the staff. The women would pass sunwise round the tipi, hug the representation of the deceased in farewell, deposit their offering, and then leave.

Some of the food would be put in a bowl, which would be placed in a hole at the base of the soul-staff, as the soul's last meal. After this had been offered to the soul, the hole in the ground was filled in, and the food – buffalo meat and wild cherry juice – was fed to four virgins waiting in the north of the tipi, the place of purity.

The tipi represents the universe. Therefore the moment that the bundle was taken from the tipi it was considered to have left the universe and returned to Wakan Tanka. The bundle itself no longer contained the soul, though it might be retained by the family. As the keeping and release of the soul were considered to benefit the tribe as well as the soul itself, the day of release would be one of celebration.

Among the Lakota, as with many tribes, the physical body of the deceased was traditionally given a 'sky burial', similar to that practised by the ancient Celts or Tibetans. It was placed on a scaffold or platform, or in a tree, where it was left for the birds of carrion and the elements to disperse to the directions. Thus the physical body returned to nature, while the spirit continued on its journey.

It might be thought that, assuming there is an immortal soul, the keeping of the soul would hold it back from progress on its path. However, it could be seen as helping the soul through what might otherwise be a difficult and confusing time, and ultimately aiding its progress, as well as helping the bereaved to come to terms with the loss of a loved one. The hugging of the soul-staff, especially, and the last meal, represent a fond but final farewell of the kind that is necessary in order for the living to let go of the deceased – without necessarily letting go of their memories.

Funeral rites varied widely from tribe to tribe. For those of the north-west coast including the Tlinglit and the Tsimshian, a *potlach* – their version of the giveaway – would help the spirit of the deceased to become free of earthly trappings. Some Alaskan and British Columbian tribes buried the dead in cemeteries, erecting huge and impressive carved totem poles to honour them. The Huron of the North-East believed that after death the soul travelled to a village in the sky. To help souls on their way, the people took part, from time to time, in Feasts of the Dead, when the living would carry the bones of the dead on their backs to a cemetery. The dead would be buried with food and many articles for their use in the afterlife.

Overall, Native Americans shared a belief in an afterlife and in reincarnation, and an assumption that life got better after death, even for those who had not lived virtuously. They regarded death as a return of the body to nature and the spirit to its own world, and saw the loss of the individual in the context of the continuing life of the family, the descendants, and the tribe as a whole.

Application

In European society, relatively little is made of the gateways from one stage of life to another. In particular we have no initiations into adulthood, apart from the Jewish Barmitzvah. Perhaps as a result of this, many young men try to prove themselves in delinquency or petty crime, or else simply fail to grow up. This seems to be less of a problem for young women, for whom biology signals a definite turning-point. In a sense, we have to make our own initiations. Try mapping the significant points in your life, and what they have taught you. What symbols would you use to represent each one?

This chapter should also make you think about your attitudes to life after death. What do you believe, and how does this affect how you live? How far can you relate to any of the beliefs and practices described in this chapter?

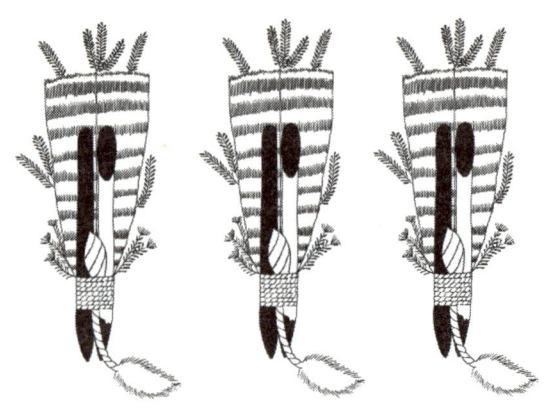

Chapter 7
The turning wheel

The song is very short because we understand so much.

[Navajo]

The previous chapter focused on the stages of the individual's path through life. This chapter deals with seasonal ceremonies that make up the turning wheel of the Native American year, and with more occasional ceremonies performed as required.

The nature and purpose of ritual

For Europeans, the word 'ritual' is frequently coupled with 'meaningless', implying that it has no practical purpose. Church ritual may serve to bring those present together in observance of a tradition which in itself gives a comforting sense of social continuity, and of personal duty done. It may also reaffirm a shared belief. However, relatively few Europeans experience ritual as something vibrant and purposeful.

True the Native American will also derive from ritual a sense of identity, belonging and continuity. However, it is much more than this. For the Native American, ritual is a purposeful, magical communication with the spirit world. It strives for harmony between heaven and earth, and it seeks the help of the spirits in achieving practical ends, such as a good harvest, abundant game or sexual fertility. A major factor in its effect is that it focuses the will of participants on a shared aim, drawing on the power of the unconscious via the medium of the imagination.

In Native American rituals, an artefact, such as the sacred pipe, actually becomes the physical focus for a concentration of spirit power when it is assembled and smoked. A dancer representing a spirit is not just play-acting: he actually becomes the spirit. Moreover, the spirit could assume a number of shapes. The Kwakiutl and Haida of the North-West, for example, believed that spirits could assume human or animal form. Dancers would wear elaborate layered masks, in which strings could be pulled to reveal successive transformations. The dancers were thought to become the transforming being they represented.

Many rituals are seasonally based. This is especially true among tribes that have traditionally practised agriculture, but even among the once nomadic Plains tribes there is still a seasonal element, based on the passage of the sun and the migration of the buffalo. Rituals are also social, with the whole tribe actively participating. Where individuals assume a special role, this benefits the tribe, as in the self-sacrifice of the Lakota Sundance, described later.

Common elements in ritual

As discussed in Chaper 4, one element common to the rituals of many tribes is the need to perform them in particular locations. The landscape is part of the people, and mirrors the heavens. It may be, too, that when generations have used a certain site for a ritual, it becomes imbued with the energy of that ritual, so that it becomes easier to perform it effectively there. Many peoples living close to the land would once have believed this. In the same way, the shrine of a god would in time become steeped in the energy of that god. Jungian psychology might explain this in terms of the effect of the site's associations on the minds of those visiting it.

Artefacts are also important in many rituals. The pipe, important for many tribes, is discussed more fully below. Many tribes make special objects for use in certain rituals, such as the Hopi's *páho* or prayer feather (see page 41), and their spirit rattles. Holy men may smoke the pipe over these objects to sanctify them. Some tribes have a holy object that they treasure and protect. The Cheyenne had a sacred arrow bundle; the Lakota have the pipe said to have been given to them by the White Buffalo Calf Woman.

Music, dance and costume harness the all important power of the imagination, and engage the emotions, without which the ritual would remain merely at the level of intellect. For many tribes, music and dance always had ritual connotations, and were never performed merely for entertainment. Drums and rattles were, and still are, used to accompany sacred songs. Large drums are pounded by as many as six people, mostly striking in unison. Smaller drums, sometimes filled with water, are used individually. Drumming embodies the continuous pulse of life, while the shape of the drum reflects the circle of life – another form of continuity. Elaborate costume and body paint may be used theatrically – as in the Hopi dances in which individuals take on the roles of kachinas (spirits).

In some cases, performers had to be extremely skilled, even though non-professionals. If a dancer stumbles in a Hopi ritual, this is thought to threaten disaster, such as a poor harvest; in some north-western tribes, if a singer forgot the words of a song, this was expected to displease the spirits and was therefore immediately punished by individuals whose job it was to rush out and beat the culprit with sticks.

Most tribes believed that their rituals were given to them either in person by a spiritual being or by a spirit manifesting in the dream or vision of an individual who would share this instruction with the tribe. Whatever view we take, this clearly confers on the ritual an authority which would help participants to take it seriously and keep it alive.

Since most tribes believed in the Six Grandfathers – the powers of the Six Directions – these feature in most rituals. Many artefacts reflect the desire to honour the directions, for example in a drum or rattle painted in their colours. Most rituals involve honouring the directions in gesture or in spoken or sung address.

In many rituals, fire represents the divine spark – spiritual energy incarnate. This echoes Greek and Jewish ideas of the sacred flame. For Native Americans, fire glows in the sacred pipe, and in the heart of the sweatlodge (see pages 61–63). The southeastern harvest festival of Busk lasted four days. On the first day, homes were cleaned, on the second and third days there was fasting, and on the fourth day, all families extinguished their fires and relit them from the shaman's central fire, as a symbol of their common origin and spiritual bond. The Hopi used the relighting of fires in a similar way (see below). Creek towns were grouped around a town square with the sacred communal fire at its centre.

Since rituals communicate with the divine, most begin with cleansing. At the very least this would involve wafting the smoke of sweetgrass or sage over the participants – known as 'smudging'. The burning of the herb is an offering in itself, and the smoke embodies the prayers rising to heaven. Micmac people use a braid of sweetgrass, a smudgestick, or a shell filled with cedar and herbs. They use a hand or feather to brush the smoke towards themselves. Smudging can be used at any special time, such as before meals. Things can be purified by smudging, too: ritual objects, gifts – even cars or computers. Purification might also involve prayer and fasting, a programme of bathing in a lake or river, or taking part in the sweatlodge ceremony.

Finally, at the heart of most rituals, and of Native American life as a whole, is the idea that relationships are constantly renewed by 'exchange'. In the Micmac language one word, *sa-syeh-wyn*, is used to mean 'exchange', 'change', 'offering', 'sacrifice' and 'trade'. For the Micmacs, the medium of exchange between humanity and the spirit world is tobacco, which is offered to the spirit world in order to receive spirit in return, and even to keep the world turning. In all ritual, then, something is given and something is received; a relationship is renewed.

The sacred pipe

The religious importance of smoking the pipe is unique to Native American culture. The pipes of the Plains tribes have bowls made of red pipestone from a quarry in south-west Minnesota. This dark red stone is supposed to be the congealed blood of the people killed during the Flood. The site is sacred, and it was generally agreed among the Plains tribes that whatever their differences they would allow each other access to it. The stem of the pipe is usually made of wood.

The Lakota describe how the original pipe was brought to them by the mysterious White Buffalo Calf Woman. The story goes that one day two braves were out hunting and saw a figure approaching. When the figure came closer they saw that it was the most beautiful woman they had ever seen. She was dressed in white buckskin and carried a bundle on her back. One of the braves desired her and declared his intentions to his friend, who tried to restrain him, since the woman was obviously holy. Undaunted, the foolish man went to the woman and both were enveloped in a white cloud. When it lifted, there was nothing left of him but a pile of bones with terrible snakes writhing among them. Both Black Elk and Lame Deer say that the snakes represent desire (and not just of the sexual kind), which eats us up from within.

The White Buffalo Calf Woman presented the sacred pipe, along with a red stone on which were seven circles, said to represent the seven campfires of the Lakota, as well as the seven rites that she was to give them. She instructed the people in the first of the rites, the Keeping of the Soul (see page 52), and told them that the remaining six would be revealed to them in due course. She then walked away, turning first into a red and brown buffalo calf, then a white buffalo, and finally a black buffalo. In some accounts she just turns into a white buffalo. At any rate, in memory of this woman the white buffalo is considered holy by all the Plains tribes, and has become a symbol of hope for many, as well as a central motif in modern Native American art.

There is also a prophecy that the old ways will return – and the earth will be saved – when four white buffalo have been born. So far there have been three, in Pine Ridge (South Dakota), Michigan (North Dakota), and Janesville (Wisconsin). This last, named Miracle, was born in 1994. At first her coat was white, then it turned red, then black, then yellow, thus echoing the four colours of the medicine wheel, and of the four races of the world. It is said that her coat will turn white again when the people of the world begin to live in harmony. The Micmac, while believing in the same origin of the pipe, believe that the world renewal will be signalled by a pair of white deer.

The pipe, said to have been given by the White Buffalo Calf Woman, has a stem made from the lower leg of a buffalo calf. It is wrapped in buffalo wool and red cloth, and has red eagle feathers, bird skins and four scalps tied to it. It has been kept by the Elk Head family of the Sans Arc (Without Bows) band of the Lakota for 14 generations. Throughout the turbulence of the last century and a half it has remained safe and not been destroyed, or even ended up in a museum or private collection.

The Native American's personal pipe can be decorated with items of personal significance. The married man's pipe has a short extension beyond the bowl, forming a 'T' shape, while a bachelor's forms an 'L'. Once smoked in prayer, the pipe is considered holy. It is used by Plains tribes, and increasingly by all Native Americans. They smoke the traditional – and non-harmful – red willow (the inner bark of the red osier dogwood, *Cornus stolonifera*), commercial pipe tobacco, or a mixture (termed *kinnikkinick*). The pipe is taken in the right hand, drawn on four times – for the directions – and passed to the left (sunwise). A more complicated ritual might involve holding it and offering it towards all six directions.

As the White Buffalo Calf Woman left the people, she sang, *Niya taniya mawani ye*: 'With visible breath I am walking'. This signifies the breath of life itself, the breath of the buffalo on a cold day, and the smoke of the pipe. In Native American thought, all these things are, in a sense, one, and the pipe contains the whole universe.

The sweatlodge

The sweatlodge ritual (*inipi* in Lakota) has achieved widespread use in North America. It has even become popular among white Americans and Europeans, especially among men's groups. In physical effect it is something like a sauna, but in symbolism and spiritual significance it is far more profound. It is used, perhaps once a week, as a ritual on its own, or as need arises as a purification before other rituals such as the vision quest or Sundance.

The lodge itself is a circular dome, like an igloo in shape, 3 or 4 metres (10 or 13 feet) across. Its frame is constructed with either 12 or 16 willow branches, the base of each being planted firmly into the ground. They are tied leaving a small hole at the top of the frame, which is like the opening in the top of a baby's skull through which spirit is supposed to enter. In the sweatlodge frame, this opening is for spirits (plural) to enter. The whole frame is covered over with quilts or blankets, and then tarpaulins are laid on top. At one time buffalo hides were used. An entrance flap is left on one side, just big enough to crawl through – thus displaying one's humility. The coverings should let in no air or light: one person inside checks; another outside adjusts. The lodge should be like a womb from which one will be reborn.

The entrance usually faces west, towards the Thunder Beings, though sometimes if faces east towards the sunrise. A shallow pit is dug in the centre of the lodge, the earth being piled a few paces from the entrance, preferably topped with a painted buffalo skull in whose eye sockets are sprigs of sage. This forms an altar, and it is considered disrespectful to walk between it and the lodge. Beyond the altar is the fire on which rocks will be heated.

The floor of the lodge was traditionally carpeted with sage, but nowadays it may just be spread with pieces of old carpet. There is no requirement to make the lodge in any way especially beautiful. After all, it is a temporary structure, not a temple.

When the rocks are hot, those taking part undress. They can wear towels, shorts, swimwear, or nothing at all. Then they crawl in, saying, 'All my relatives' (*Mitakuye oyasin* in Lakota; *No-o-go-mach* in Micmac), usually filling the lodge in a sunwise direction. The leader, whether a medicine man or woman, or just the person taking overall responsibility, sits just inside the flap, to the south. Then the helper, whose place is next to the flap, takes rocks from the fire with a pitchfork and hands them in. The leader flips the fork so that the rocks land in the pit, positioning them, if necessary, with deer antlers. When the rocks – probably six of them – are in, the helper undresses and enters. The leader and helper reach out to a bucket of water, bring it in, and close the flap. Sprigs of cedar, sage or sweetgrass may be thrown on the hot rocks for fragrance and blessing.

The leader may now address the group about the ritual's purpose, or may pray, or sing. He then pours water on the rocks, and steam fills the lodge. (Among north-eastern tribes the leader might splash water on with a cedar branch.) There may be drumming and singing. It becomes very hot, and a first-timer may feel a little anxious or claustrophobic, not knowing just how hot it is going to get. But a good leader will take this into account. In addition, anyone may at any time say *Mitakuye oyasin*, and the flap will be opened for air. People may talk and joke while the flap is open, but not while it is shut. Although it is good to try to relax into the heat, the ritual is not meant to be an endurance test.

There may be several batches of hot rocks and openings of the flap. The leader will also start a round of prayers. Individuals pray aloud, especially for others, taking turns and saying *Mitakuye oyasin* when finished. Some people may see or sense spirits, and have messages to relay to the group. What people say is strictly confidential. When the sweatlodge is over there may be a meal — usually a cheerful occasion — with everyone feeling cleansed and united by the shared sweatlodge.

The seasons

Most tribes had, and in many cases still observe, rituals closely linked to the seasons. These would be timed by a combination of solar and lunar phases, as indeed is Easter in Europe. The Plateau tribes, for example, greeted the start of the berry season with a Grizzly Dance, singing to the Bear Spirit at an altar incorporating a grizzly bear skull. Those near rivers, like tribes further west, had a ritual to welcome the salmon. This included prayer and silent feasting.

Perhaps the most elaborate seasonal rites are those of the Hopi. Their year begins around 1 November. Interestingly this coincides with Samhain, the festival which begins the Celtic year. Both cultures see the time of apparent dying down as a birth — life in death. Another feature of the Hopi ceremonial year is that each ceremony performed on earth is thought to be performed by the spirits during the corresponding month below the earth.

However, since the earth and spirit world mirror each other, the seasons are reversed. Hence when the first winter ceremony on earth, Powamu, is observed, preparations are made for the summer ceremony of Niman Kachina, because this is currently being observed by the spirits. This mirroring echoes traditional Lakota practice (see page 20).

Wúwuchim

This is the first of the three winter ceremonies forming the bedrock of the Hopi year. These portray the three phases of creation, which correspond to the phases of dawn: the purplish pre-dawn light in which man is first outlined; the yellow dawn light revealing man's breath; and the red glow in which man is fully revealed. Hopis are initiated into various religious societies, and Wúwuchim is led by the Two Horn society, which is said to have knowledge of the previous worlds as well as this one – whereas the knowledge of the One Horn society is limited to this world. The ceremony represents an appeal to the spirit world for the germination of all life forms on earth.

Wúwuchim consists of an eight day preparation period followed by eight days of secret rituals conducted by four separate religious societies in their *kivas* (ceremonial chambers), concluding with a public dance. The first ritual is the New-Fire ceremony, which acts out the dawn of creation. Before dawn, a new fire is kindled. It is fed with coal and prayers to Másaw, god of the underworld, who uses solar power to keep his volcanic fires burning. Brands from this new fire are used to light fires in the other kivas. This ritual symbolically warms the crust of the earth, while later rituals enact the germination of seed, growth and ripening of crops.

Next, all roads into the village are closed with a line of sacred cornmeal, sealing it off from evil. No one dares cross these lines for fear of dying within four years. Just one path is left open for spirits to enter – a tortuous one on which a guard is posted. The roads stay closed for the 'Night of the Washing of the Hair', during which members of the One Horn society patrol the village armed with lances. Traditionally it was their duty to stab and dismember any human they encountered. Priests would carry bits of the body in the different directions as far as they could travel that night, then bury them there. Members of the Two Horn society, more highly initiated, and therefore more compassionate, were duty-bound to rush to the intruder's aid.

The climax of this night is an initiation of young men in which they are surrounded by spirit figures in a kiva, and at the signal of a rock covering the fire pit, must all scramble naked up the ladders leading out of the kiva, simulating emergence from the world before it is destroyed. Further rituals involve dancing, and the smoking of the pipe, accompanied by seven songs that describe the beginnings and evolution of life on earth. These are sung at night, and must be completed before the Pleiades disappear.

Soyál

This represents the second phase of creation. Its fuller name is *Soyálangwul*, 'Establishing life anew for all the world' – through germination. It takes place at the winter solstice, when the sun begins his journey towards his summer house. It lasts twenty days, including eight days preparation and a four day rabbit hunt.

During Soyál, the first spirit of the year, the Soyál Kachina, appears, wearing a turquoise helmet and white robe. He staggers like a toddler. The next day the Mastop Kachina appears, in a black mask, body painted black with white handprints, an animal skin kilt, and wildcat fur shoes. Three white stars on either side of his head represent Orion's Belt, from which region he is supposed to have come. His black body represents the earth; grass around his throat represents the plant world; the skin kilt represents the animal kingdom; the handprints represent human impact on the world. He grabs a woman from the crowd and simulates intercourse with her, representing both human procreation and fertility in nature and crops.

The complex and esoteric rituals include one in which the Soyál chief dances energetically to each of the four primary directions with a spinning buckskin shield representing the sun. The lower half of the shield is painted blue, the top-right quarter is painted red, and the top-left quarter is painted yellow. Eyes and a mouth are marked in black, and a black strip outlined in white runs down from the forehead. The face is fringed with human hair stained red for the sun's rays. The colours represent the directions. Those present concentrate on helping the sun to regain his strength after the near-death of the solstice.

Powamu

This 16-day ceremony represents the final phase of creation. Beans are planted in the kivas. These are encouraged to germinate by stoves kept burning round the clock, and by kachinas who visit the kivas and dance to help their 'children', the beans. Every four years the Powamu ceremony includes the initiation of children (see page 49). After this the Crow Mother Kachina appears and sings the story of the Kachina Clan's migration around the village. The bean plants are cut and tied into bundles, and at sunrise, kachinas deliver them to all homes in the village with presents for the children, including a kachina doll for girls and moccasins for boys.

Other Hopi ceremonies

We have looked very briefly at what are in fact the enormously complex three main Hopi ceremonies. There are others, including the summer solstice Niman Kachina, when the kachinas (spirits) go home for the winter – which to Hopis is the time between the summer and winter solstices. The Flute ceremony is in mid-August and aims to bring the last of the season's rains and ripen the crops. It includes a re-telling of the story of the Hopi emergence into the present world. It is alternated with the better-known Snake-Antelope ceremony. In this ceremony, participants first sit while freshly caught snakes roam freely over their bodies; the snakes are said to prefer the holiest participants. Later they perform a public dance holding the snakes – some venomous – in their mouths. The snakes represent what Hindus call the *kundalini* energy, which lies coiled in the Muladhara chakra at the base of the spine. The fact that participants remain calm and suffer no injuries testifies to their presence of mind and attunement to the natural world. After the ceremony the snakes are taken out in armfuls and released to the four directions.

The Sundance

Many Europeans have heard of the Sundance and imagine it to be a form of torture, or at least of self-torture; others think it is a test of manhood. Many assume that it died out years ago. True it was at one time banned by the US Government, and regarded by whites as barbaric. However, it has continued, at first in secret, then openly, and many young Native Americans now pledge themselves to dance, at least once in their lives.

As for the idea of the Sundance as self-torture or an endurance test, all teachers make it clear that the Sundance is an intensely spritual practice undertaken for the communal good. For some young men, no doubt an element of *machismo* is involved, but the real point of the dance is self-sacrifice for others.

The nearest thing in modern Europe to the Sundance, at least on the physical level, is the considerably less daunting custom of Maypole dancing. This is similar in two respects: the participants dance around a central tree, or pole, representing the Tree of Life (also like the Norse world-tree, Yggdrasil); they are attached by strings (or ribbons) to the top of the tree, or pole, representing the rays of the sun, as well as the links between the individual and the central source of life. It might be added that both take place once a year, in time with the solar cycle: the Lakota Sundance traditionally took place at the annual summer gathering of the tribe in the Black Hills.

For Plains tribes, the tree is a carefully chosen cottonwood, which must be felled with a new axe by four virgins, and which must not be allowed to touch the ground as it falls. The tree is carried by twenty bearers to the Sundance ground, where it is inserted in a hole in the ground filled with buffalo fat. At one time there would have been a great rush of warriors racing to be first to touch the erected tree, 'counting coup' on it as if it were an honoured enemy.

Some Plateau tribes practised a relatively undemanding form of the Sundance in which young men danced before a Sundance doll for a day and a night. However, the traditional Lakota Sundance is altogether more challenging. Those who have pledged to dance – and this is a personal choice – purify themselves in the sweatlodge. Then they dance for three days and nights, going without food, water and sleep. They blow on eagle bone whistles. Spectators watch from a lodge of pine boughs around the Sundance circle.

On the fourth day, dancers have two skewers of cherry wood or eagle bone thrust through their chests. These are attached to rawhide cords which run to the top of the Sundance tree, and the dancers must lean back on them, praying and blowing their whistles, staring at the sun, perhaps all day, until eventually the skewers pull right through their flesh and they are free. There are other ways for them to be attached to the cords, such as through the back, but the chest method, called 'gazing at the sun leaning', is the most common.

The thinking behind the Sundance sacrifice is that all we have to offer Wakan Tanka that we can call our own is our flesh. Participants may take part for a particular reason, for example, to give strength to a son recovering from alcoholism. Women do not dance, but they may cut pieces of flesh from their arms. Lakota medicine man Lame Deer says that Christians believe in redemption through Christ's suffering, whereas the Lakota believe that it is up to every one of us to help each other.

Personal rituals

To talk about a *personal* Native American ritual is perhaps to use a misnomer, in that all Native American rituals to some extent involve the tribe. However, there are some rituals that neither involve the tribe in a collective, seasonal concern, such as a harvest or solstice, nor mark the gateways through which all or most individuals pass from birth to death. One example is the Lakota *Hunka* ceremony.

This ceremony is sometimes called 'the making of relatives', which in itself is a recurring theme. Native American culture tends towards interrelatedness; European culture pulls in the opposite direction, towards individualism and the breaking of family ties. The Hunka ceremony, still common today, is used for an older person to adopt a younger person, as if parent and child, or for people of the same age to become siblings. In the former case the older person is called the Ate Hunka and the younger the Hunka; in the latter, both are Hunka to each other. The obligations formed are taken very seriously – more so, for example, than is usually the case with European godparents. Hunkas must help each other whatever the cost, in all situations. Traditionally they were also obliged to avenge a fellow Hunka killed in battle.

The Hunka ceremony itself is conducted by a medicine man, who waves horse tails – or bunches of horse hair – over the pair. There is prayer, singing of Hunka songs, smoking of the pipe, and offerings of corn and meat. The two candidates are tied together, leg to leg and arm to arm. They are entitled to wear red stripes on their faces. According to Black Elk, the ceremony originated as a peace-maker between the Lakota and their enemies, the Ree tribe – closely related to the Pawnee – when the Lakota had unwittingly taken the Ree's sacred corn and the Ree came to ask for it back.

Whatever its origins, the concept of Hunka is one that should inspire us to better and more supportive friendships – perhaps even more important to us today as family ties are eroded by our lifestyles and by the geographical mobility demanded by the modern labour market.

The giveaway

The giveaway ceremony, known among the north-west tribes as the *potlach*, is found in various forms across North America. Since it is based on giving away one's material possessions, sometimes in great quantities and even to the point where one has almost nothing left, it goes right against the grain of European materialism and consumerism.

The giveaway is not usually presided over by a medicine man. Rather it is organized by the family. Moreover, although it has spiritual consequences, it has more to do with an eschewal of material ties, and a desire to benefit or honour others, than with communication with the spirit world. However, in the North-West a family or individual might spend a year preparing for the potlach, and it would be attended by elaborate ceremony, dance and song. Interestingly, north-western tribal culture has traditionally encouraged the accumulation of personal wealth to a far greater exent than elsewhere. This wealth would confer great prestige. There was also a strong element of competition between high-ranking individuals in how much each could afford to give. One positive result of this was that wealth became recycled, and many of the poorer villagers benefited. Here, as elsewhere, there are comparisons to be made with the Celts, whose aristocracy competed in feast-giving.

For all Native American tribes the giveaway would involve giving presents to particular individuals, thus forming a relationship with them. Present-giving more generally is of great importance to Native Americans, because it establishes or renews a relationship. Perhaps we should think of that when we rush out on Christmas Eve to buy socks for someone because we've 'got to get them something'! Many Algonquin people still have giveaway ceremonies on special occasions. The person receiving the gift wears it or holds it aloft in the pow-wow dance. Often they keep the gift for a year and then give it away to someone else – not because they want to get rid of it, but because giving and receiving is a continuous process that is simply in harmony with the constant exchanges of matter and energy in the natural world.

The Ghost dance

One of the most tragic episodes of Native American history centres on the Ghost dance. The story begins in the late 1880s. Almost all Native Americans were now eking out a meagre existence, confined to reservations, dependent on inadequate and irregular government supplies, their culture severely threatened. On 1 January 1889, during a solar eclipse, a Paiute medicine man named Wovoka had a vision in which he was taken up to heaven and saw all the people who had been killed by the whites now living happily as they had done before the whites had come. He was taught five songs, and a circle dance – the Ghost dance.

Wovoka began to preach, and soon won a huge following in his native South-West. Native Americans from other areas heard that he was the messiah, and travelled to hear him, among them several Lakotas, including Short Bull and Kicking Bear. Suddenly there was a religion uniting tribes who had formerly been enemies. Wovoka taught that if people sung the songs and danced the dance, they would see their dead relatives. Moreover, a great flood would drown the whites. People who failed to dance and believe the teaching would shrink or turn to wood and be burned in fires. According to another teaching transmitted by Short Bull and Kicking Bear, who became leaders of the dance among the Lakota, the earth would roll up like a carpet, revealing its former glory. The buffalo would return and the whites would vanish.

The Ghost dance religion was non-violent. Wovoka taught brotherly love and tolerance. The dance was a mystical ritual in which many participants had visions of heaven and of lost relatives. One of its songs contains the line: 'The spotted eagle is coming to carry me away.' The spotted eagle is a symbol of the sun, and of Wakan Tanka. Thus the line implies mystical union with the infinite. Many of Wovoka's followers who had encountered Christianity considered him to be Christ come again. Despite the peaceful nature of the Ghost dance, it led to the tragedy of the Wounded Knee massacre, already described in Chapter 1.

In 1973 members of the AIM (American Indian Movement) occupied Wounded Knee. Their spiritual leader, medicine man Leonard Crow Dog, believed that Short Bull and Kicking Bear had misinterpreted Wovoka's message. To Crow Dog, the Ghost dance was about keeping traditions alive by creating a link with the ancestors and the past. He led a Ghost dance at Wounded Knee, and has continued to do this on the Rosebud Reservation.

Application

For the European there are perhaps two main lessons to learn from the Sundance. One is the willingness to sacrifice for the sake of others; the other is the ability to endure some degree of physical hardship. Though some whites have participated in a Sundance, few will want to take on such physical pain. However, we can try to develop equanimity towards the physical discomforts that routinely come to us, allowing them to teach us that although we *have* bodies, we in fact are *not* our bodies. The body that feels the pain or discomfort will one day be discarded; the spirit lives on. One further possible lesson is that sometimes we must suffer in order to break away from a person or situation — an emotional parallel to the way in which the Sundancers literally tear themselves free.

As a materialistic society, we also have much to learn from the giveaway. Most of us are quite reluctant to give away the fruits of our labours. But giving can help to break burdensome ties to the material world, and to encourage a sense of plenty, as well as developing a relationship with those to whom we give. Give something away now!

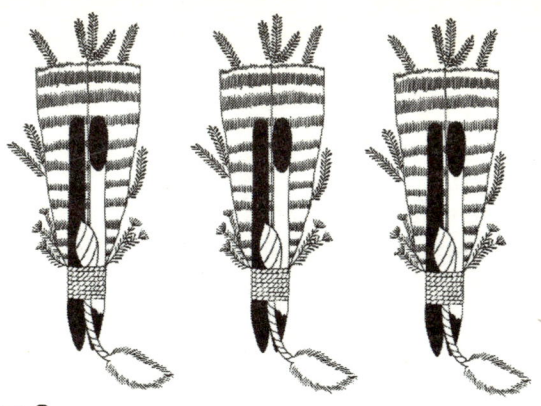

Chapter 8
Codes of conduct

Thoughts are like arrows: once released, they strike their mark. Guard them well or one day you may be your own victim.

[Navajo]

All societies have their moral codes and models for personal conduct. The Romans, for example, in common with Japanese warriors, thought it better to commit suicide than suffer the dishonour of defeat. Christians and Jews, on the other hand, guided by their religious teachings, see suicide as one of the worst possible crimes.

There were major differences in moral codes between Native Americans and the incoming white culture. Moreover, as far as the Native American could see, whites did not even respect the morality they professed to believe in. As Plenty Coups, an Absaroka of the Plains, says:

They spoke very loudly when they said their laws were made for everybody; but we soon learned that although they expected us to keep them, they thought nothing of breaking them themselves. They told us not to drink whisky, yet they made it themselves and traded it to us for furs and robes until both were nearly gone. Their Wise Ones said we might have their religion ... we saw that the white man did not take his religion any more seriously than he did his laws, and that he kept both of them just behind him, like Helpers, to use when they might do him good. ...These were not our ways. We kept the laws we made and lived our religion. We have never been able to understand the white man, who fools nobody but himself.[1]

There was also a major difference in the way the two cultures regarded infringements of their codes. A Native American avoided crime not only because of the fear of social stigma, or because of conscience, but because crime created an imbalance in the world, a disruption of spiritual harmony. The tribe would have to consider what the wrong-doer could do to restore this balance.

The moral codes of Native Americans vary from tribe to tribe. However, there are broad similarities, outlined below.

Speaking from the heart

It may be that a society becomes more adept at lying, and less attached to truth, when it becomes literate. Perhaps the act of putting something down in writing enables the individual to distance himself from his own words. The illiterate Celts valued honest dealing, and scorned tackling an enemy by lies and treachery. The Romans, on the other hand, had no such scruples.

The Anishinabe have a saying: 'It is less a problem to be poor than to be dishonest.' Not all Native Americans are honest without exception, but history suggests that they value truth highly, knowing that Wakan Tanka sees all. They rarely make promises, as distinct from statements of intent, as they are unnecessary. However, a treaty, sanctified by the pipe represents a promise to Wakan Tanka. Native Americans were therefore astonished and embittered by the cavalier fashion in which the whites violated their own written treaties, which they claimed to take so seriously.

Like the Celts, Native Americans had many orators among them, the Nez Percé Chief Joseph being one:

Good words will not give me back my children. Good words will not give my people good health and stop them from dying. Good words will not get my people a home where they can live in peace and take care of themselves. I am tired of talk that comes to nothing. It makes my heart sick when I remember all the good words and all the broken promises.[2]

To Native American thinking, true oratory comes 'from the heart' and from personal experience. This is also seen as the secret of relationships. Some Algonquin people call truth 'our connection to the earth': it is that important. To the Algonquins, truth bonds society, while dishonesty pulls it apart. To speak from the heart, rather than to use words manipulatively or diplomatically, takes courage. We can but try!

This attitude to truth has not generally been shared by the white man. In fact, the whole history of relations between whites and Native Americans has been one of lies and broken promises. Sadly this history has left a legacy of suspicion. That the Hollywood Western line, 'White man speak with forked tongue,' has become such a cliché is ironic, because it is so true in terms of the Native American's experience.

Connected to the idea of the sanctity of the word is the sanctity of names. A Native American personal name comes from a vision or dream, and is thought to have power. The same applies to the names of places and things in nature. Young Chief, a Cayuse, says:

God named the roots that he should feed the Indians on: the water speaks the same way. ... the grass says the same thing. ... The Earth and water and grass say God has given our names and we are told those names: neither the Indians [n]or the Whites have a right to change those names.[3]

One also finds in Native American oral traditions a concept of what Buddhists would call Right Speech. This is not just basic honesty, but an avoidance of idle gossip, particularly of the malicious kind. In this tradition, all words have power, and should therefore be treated with respect.

Whose land?

The traditional Native American attitude towards personal property is not entirely different from that of the white man. Individuals have possessed more, or less, property, and have gained status by what they owned. They have traded for horses and goods, and sought to get good deals for themselves. In the northwest there has even been a culture in which some individuals owned much more than they needed.

On the other hand, most traditional Native Americans would share personal good fortune with their extended family, and even with their tribe, and there would have been no Native American community in which some feasted while others starved. This attitude survives today, although one sometimes hears Native Americans complaining that people are becoming more like the white man – 'out for themselves'.

While Native Americans, like Europeans, have always had personal property, the attitudes of the two cultures towards land ownership have always been opposed. The idea that land can be bought and sold, fenced in and owned by individuals, is alien to Native American thinking, although all tribes had some sense of their having special rights to hunt or cultivate their homeland. There were territorial disputes, but prompted by need, not greed. Moreover, these disputes, which tended to result in skirmishes rather than wars, became far worse with the instability caused by the white man pushing the tribes westwards, and by the introduction of horses and guns.

The Native American attitude to the sale of land is eloquently put by Crowfoot, a member of the Blackfoot tribe:

Our land is more valuable than your money. It will last forever. It will not even perish by the flames of fire. As long as the sun shines and the waters flow, this land will be here to give life to men and animals. We cannot sell the lives of men and animals. It was put here for us by the Great Spirit and we cannot sell it because it does not belong to us. You can count your money and burn it within the nod of a buffalo's head, but only the Great Spirit can count the grains of sand and the blades of grass on the plains. As a present to you, we will give you anything we have that you can take with you; but the land, never.[4]

The warrior code

For a Lakota warrior, the four cardinal virtues were courage, fortitude, wisdom and generosity. Other Plains tribes had similar codes. It was desirable for both sexes to be brave, though normally only men were involved in battle and hunting large game such as buffalo. Women would make much of a man who had excelled in battle, and encouraged war parties and horse-raids. However, we must remember that war to these people was rarely on a large scale.

In fact war often had more to do with demonstrating bravery than with forming an efficient killing machine. This is shown by the custom of 'counting coup', whereby a warrior would gain prestige by riding up to an enemy and touching him with a special stick. Since the enemy would probably be trying to kill him, this was considered very brave. There was even a system of grading whereby a warrior would get different levels of prestige for 'counting coup' on the enemy's person, or on his horse, his tipi, and so on. Some Lakota saddles even had bells on, to emphasize the fact that the rider was so brave that he had no need to sneak up on the enemy unheard.

The Apache attitude was somewhat different. They now have a reputation as aggressive plunderers. However, this stems partly from an early Spanish Indian policy that singled them out for persecution and set other tribes against them, forcing them to live by predation, and partly from Hollywood seizing on them as a symbol of the hated 'savage'. The reality is that a traditional Apache raid's main aim was to avoid the enemy. To this purpose they even conducted rituals to confer invisibility. They had no warrior societies and did not take scalps, possibly because they had a taboo against touching the dead. When forced to defend themselves against white persecution, their speciality was the ambush rather than the head-on confrontation. Geronimo, who became a symbol of the Apache 'scourge', only wanted his people to be left in peace.

Although a warrior was concerned to obtain personal status, behind this was a desire to bring honour to his family and to protect the tribe. Among some tribes, including the Lakota, respect for the warrior – or the veteran as he is now often called – is very much alive. At pow-wows – large social gatherings featuring dance and music – there are often dances and speeches honouring veterans who have fought in the US armed forces. This is a little puzzling, given that these forces are the institutional descendants of the much-hated US Cavalry, fighting what essentially are white man's wars – and often against people who have much in common with the Native Americans, such as the Vietnamese. It also sits awkwardly with the fact that many Lakotas fly the US flag on their houses – not out of patriotism, but because they consider it to have become theirs when they took it from General Custer at the Battle of the Little Big Horn. It seems that courage itself is considered more important than ideology.

The role of women

In the past, some Native American men had more than one wife, if they could afford it. In general it seems that they did their best to treat their wives equally, and the reports suggest that perhaps the women even liked this arrangement. Certainly it was a point of pride for every man to provide for his wife – or wives – and children. George Catlin reports that women in the tribes he encountered were never ill-treated: there was no domestic violence – although this is a problem in the run-down, depressed reservation communities of today. He also asserts that although women worked hard preparing buffalo hides, gathering roots and fruit, cooking, and so on, they were not exploited in the way that white women often were: they were simply following the division of labour. The men took charge of protecting the camp and hunting.

Native American women nowadays, if one can generalize, are strong and assertive. In accordance with tradition, they are particularly powerful in the home, and are generally regarded as the heads of the families. In many tribes the woman is thought of as the home-owner, and in theory can divorce a bad husband simply by throwing his personal possessions out of the house.

In many Native American tribes, women had a great deal of power. They owned horses, and added to their herds by trading.

There were also women warriors, such as the Cheyenne's Buffalo Calf Road Woman, who rode into battle and rescued her brother. Running Eagle of the Blackfoot tribe was famous as a warrior, war chief and holy woman. The Apache, Lakota and Crow also had notable women warriors. This, coupled with the fact that Plains tribes, at least, accepted homosexuality, regarding it more or less as a third sex – and even one whose members had special mystical powers – suggests an attitude to gender differences in which individual inclinations were ultimately more important than stereotypes.

Women had their special spiritual and cultural roles. Among the Plateau tribes it was the woman's responsibility to keep the history of the family using a 'time ball' of twine knotted to mark important events. Women of the Flathead and Kootenai tribes formed the mystical Crazy Owl society to ward off disease.

Women also had political power. There were individual women leaders, and many tribes were matrilinear, especially in the North-West. One Plains myth says that woman was created first to make the right choices in the life-path, and that man was created to accompany her. Among the north-eastern woodland tribes, girl babies were especially welcome, as they would carry on the matrilinear line. In the South-East, also mostly matrilinear, clan matriarchs had the ultimate authority, although they appointed a male council to handle day-to-day administration.

Old and young

Native Americans living traditional lives often lived to a great age, but were never marginalized as they often are in industrial societies. On the contrary, many tribes have a tradition of what has been called 'gerontocracy', or government by the old, perhaps reflecting their Asian roots. Modern China still embodies this tendency in government.

Native American communities, on the other hand, tend to be democratic. The old do not necessarily have great political power by virtue of age, but their wisdom and experience is respected, and they are treated accordingly. In some communities it is customary to greet or serve food to people in descending order of age, and at many gatherings elders are given offerings or gifts. The Cree have a saying: 'Never sit while your elders stand.' At modern-day pow-wows there are dances 'to honour the elders', during which spectators are expected to stand. It is considered a compliment to call an old woman 'Grandmother', and to ask 'how many winters' she has seen.

Children were often brought up largely by grandparents, parents being occupied with work and providing, so older people were never redundant. The old had much to teach the young, and often had a special relationship with them. For example, among the Iroquois it was an old woman who led the children around the village at the midwinter festival in a kind of 'trick or treat' expedition, dancing, singing and asking for presents.

Since couples usually married young, many people would live to be great-grandparents – and to see seven generations including their own. The wisdom of such an elder, whom the Micmacs call *geezegodwit* – meaning 'he is so old that he is bent over like an old pine tree ready to fall' – would be especially valued. At the same time, the elder would traditionally be preparing mentally and spiritually to leave this world. Even today one meets very old Native Americans who, while full of love, are so unattached to this world that they seem about to blow away into the world of spirit.

Native Americans see children as coming fresh from the spirit world, or from Wakan Tanka. They might in some cases be reincarnations of ancestors – reinforcing the link between old and young. They are usually treated with respect, and even indulged. Even in a modern home one might find a two-year-old drumming and singing loudly while the adults talk unconcernedly over the noise.

Children's play would reflect the skills they would eventually have to develop. Many carefully made dolls and even play tipis – like dolls' houses – made to perfect scale, survive from the nineteenth century. Plains girls would first be given a 'rag' doll (while still young enough to imagine its finer details), and then a more realistic one when they were older – and closer to the time when they would have a real baby. Boys would play a game that involved aiming a spear through a moving hoop, training them to hit a moving target. Among the Apache, on the other hand, boys and girls would have the same basic physical training, as both would have to learn to look after themselves.

Socializing and hospitality

Among most tribes there are strong codes of hospitality. A Navajo proverb says: 'Assume that a visitor is tired, hungry and thirsty, and act accordingly.' A visitor will normally be offered food — and offence may be taken if it is refused! There are many stories of tribes giving generous help and sustenance to early white explorers — before the whites became an obvious threat. Some north-eastern families still honour the tradition of keeping a pot of soup simmering at all times for hungry visitors.

Native Americans, while having a strong individuality, have always been sociable in the strongest sense of the word, depending on each other in so many ways, and putting the tribe and family first, and themselves last. Celebrations have always been large-scale affairs, and the biggest of these now are the annual pow-wows. These are great social events, usually for a whole tribe, but sometimes intertribal. They focus on music and dance — especially dance. Dancing is thought to be particularly instructive for young people, teaching them boundaries, and to express their individuality within the form of a tradition. Nowadays much of the dancing is competitive, and there are big prizes. However, behind this there is still a feeling that the social occasion is the most important thing, and that ultimately even the social dances are spiritual. Such dances are even used as a form of group post-traumatic stress therapy for war veterans.

Democracy

Tribes vary enormously in this respect. Any form of highly centralized power, or dictatorship, was relatively rare, though it did occur in the South-East. In many tribes there was a hierarchy, often with elders having the most power. In the North-West the hierarchy was based on material wealth. However, overall there was a strong element of democracy, and of every individual having a right to express an opinion. In some tribes there would be formal methods for ensuring this, such as the 'talking stick' or 'talking feather', which would be passed round, each person having the right to speak while they held it. So advanced was the outlook of many tribes encountered by the first settlers, that they had a significant influence on the thinking of men like Thomas Jefferson in the eighteenth century, and on the Declaration of Independence.

The Cherokee and Creeks especially had sophisticated systems of government based on elected councils, free speech and consultation. Tribal officials of the Eastern Cherokee belonged either to the White Peace Organization or the Red War Organization. The former governed religious ceremonies and ran criminal and civil courts; the latter was in charge of enlisting warriors, purification rites before and after battle, the treatment of the wounded, and of course the actual fighting.

Application

Native American views and codes of behaviour should make us reassess our attitudes towards:

- **Honesty**: Make a list of the times that you have lied or been 'economical with the truth' during the last week. If you can't think of any, go back a month, or a year. Then consider the times when you have not been exactly dishonest, but have not spoken from the heart. Think of what you might say to people if you did, and what the results might be.
- **Land ownership**: Most of us do not own acres of land. However, we can put pressure on government to recognize that land ownership is really stewardship. The 'right to roam' is a freedom of which Native Americans would heartily approve. We have an obligation to future generations, and to the land itself, to protect it from exploitation and ruin. Join an environmental group.
- **Family and community**: Many of us have rather flimsy ties with family and community. Consider how you can improve these, and what the benefits might be for all concerned. Think especially of the elderly, what they deserve, and what they have to offer. Whatever age people are, allow them a basic respect even if you do not like them. Be prepared to hear and consider their views.

Conclusion

This book has been an attempt to convey both the diversity and common ground of Native American culture. Native Americans themselves tend to identify with their tribe first, and with the larger Native American population second. This view has been encouraged by reservation life, since each reservation is a pocket of land held by a single tribe. At the same time, as noted in Chapter 1, there has since the 1970s been a growth in 'pan-Indianism' – a recognition of shared beliefs, values and problems.

Some Native Americans view non-Native interest in their culture and spiritual practices with suspicion, feeling that both may be diluted, cheapened or exploited if revealed to non-Natives. Some simply feel that people should seek spiritual enlightenment through their own culture.

Other Native Americans, however, acknowledge that they do have something special to teach not only to those of their own people who have spiritually lost their way, but to non-Natives disenchanted with materialism. One such teacher is Lakota medicine man Wallace Black Elk, who regards himself as a spiritual descendant of the Black Elk referred to elsewhere in this book.

A major lesson is that: 'We are all relatives' – human, animals, plants, and even rocks and stones. In the Native American view we are all children of Mother Earth, and we will suffer if we fail to act accordingly. A closely related lesson is that we should see ourselves as stewards of land, not outright owners who can do whatever we like with it. Native American attitudes towards truthfulness, and to time, would also benefit Western materialistic society.

One aspect of the Native outlook that is coincidentally gaining ground in the wider society is 'holistic thinking', that integrates the left and right brain, logic and abstraction with intuition and symbolism. This integration is seen, for example, in the developing art of storytelling, an art which has never died out in Native communities.

Many Native American teachers are concerned with keeping the traditions pure, but since it is impossible for non-Natives to 'convert' to Native religion, it is inevitable that non-Natives will be influenced by it rather than taking it on wholesale. Native Americans are rightly scornful of anyone 'playing at Indians'. However, non-Natives can absorb and apply Native wisdom, while respectfully leaving the more culturally exclusive practices – such as the Sundance – to the Native Americans.

One way in which non-Natives are likely to absorb the influence of Native thought is through the arts. Oscar Howe is one acclaimed artist who has brilliantly expressed a Native American outlook on canvas. There are also outstanding sculptors, such as Larry and Alfred DeCoteau of the Turtle Mountain Ojibway, ceramicists such as Randall Blaze (Oglala Sioux), and craft-based artists such as Claire Packard (Yankton Sioux). Native music is also very much alive, in forms ranging from traditional to rap and New Age. In the realm of words, Louise Erdrich is one of a number of Native American novelists, while Tomson Highway is an award-winning Cree playwright.

One interesting media development is that many Native American communities have embraced the Internet, and there are a number of very informative Native websites. The Internet seems to be a technological expression of the Native belief in interconnectedness. Here, perhaps, is a successful marriage of two cultures, giving hope that as we go forward into the twenty-first century we will see Native American wisdom winning non-Native respect and playing its part in creating a more enlightened global community.

REFERENCES

Please refer to Bibliography for full bibliographical details.

Chapter 3
[1] Miller, p. 231.
[2] Debo, p. 3.
[3] Navajo Religion on **http://www.xpressweb.com/zionpark** Visit for more information.
[4] ibid.
[5] Quoted in Goodman, p. 15.
[6] Walker, pp. 138–139.

Chapter 4
[1] Lame Deer, pp. 211-212
[2] For information on the Micmac language and people I am indebted to Evan T. Pritchard (also co-author of *Introductory Guide to Micmac Words and Phrases*).
[3] Quoted from exhibit label in Northern Plains Tribal Arts Gallery, Sioux Falls.
[4] Neihardt, p. 40.
[5] Information from Sams' chapter in Matthews, pp. 110–118.

Chapter 5
[1] Lame Deer, p. 109.
[2] Goodman, p. 17.
[3] Catlin, p. 157.

Chapter 6
[1] Lame Deer, p. 146.
[2] Brown, Joseph Epes, p. 11.

Chapter 8
[1] Miller, pp. 231–233.
[2] ibid., p. 342.
[3] ibid., p. 333.
[4] ibid., p. 234.

BIBLIOGRAPHY

* Brown, Dee, *Bury My Heart at Wounded Knee*, Vintage, London, 1991
* Brown, Joseph Epes (ed.), *The Sacred Pipe*, Penguin, Harmondsworth, 1972
* Catlin, George, *Life Among the Indians*, Bracken Books, 1996
* Debo, Angie, *A History of the Indians of the United States*, Pimlico, London, 1995
* Erdoes, R., and Ortiz, A., *American Indian Myths and Legends*, Pimlico, London, 1997
* Goodman, Ronald, *Lakota Star Knowledge*, Sinte Gleska University, Rosebud, 1992
* Hand, Floyd Looks for Buffalo, *Learning Journey on the Red Road*, Learning Journey Communications, Toronto, 1998
* Josephy, Alvin M., *The Indian Heritage of America*, Penguin, Harmondsworth, 1975
* Lame Deer and R. Erdoes, *Lame Deer, Seeker of Visions*, Simon & Schuster, 1972
* Matthews, John (ed.), *The World Atlas of Divination*, Bullfinch Press, Boston, 1992
* Miller, Lee, *From the Heart*, Pimlico, London 1997
* Neihardt, John G., *Black Elk Speaks*, Abacus, London, 1974
* Pritchard, Evan T., *No Word for Time*, Council Oak Books, Tulsa, 1997
* Sherman, Josepha, *Indian Tribes of North America*, Richard Todd, 1996
* Stolzman, Fr. William (First Eagle), *How to Take Part in Lakota Ceremonies*, Tipi Press, Chamberlain, 1995
* Versluis, Arthur, *The Elements of Native American Traditions*, Element Books, 1993

* Walker, James R., *Lakota Belief and Ritual*, University of Nebraska, Lincoln, 1991
* Waters, Frank, *The Book of the Hopi*, Ballantine Books, New York, 1969
* Zimmerman, Larry J., *Native North America*, Macmillan, London, 1996

Websites

http://www.geocities.com/Athens/Acropolis/5579/dakota.html
http://www.takhota.com/culture.htm
http://www.xpressweb.com/zionpark

Index

agriculture 28
Algonquin 70, 75
American Indian Movement (AIM) 71
Apache
   beliefs 18
   resistance to whites 3, 77
   solstice observation 20
Aphrodite, compared with Wohpe 6
animal spirits 26–7
Arapaho 46–47
archetypes 26–27
arts
   Native American 38–42
   attitude to 42–3

Bear Butte 18
bereavement 52
'Big Bang' theory 10
Big Foot 3
Big Horn Medicine Wheel 20
Black Elk 32, 33
Black Elk, Wallace 83
Black Hills 20–3
Blessingway chant 11–12
Buddhism 27, 30–31, 51, 75
buffalo 11, 15, 23, 26–27, 28, 60
Buffalo Calf Road Woman 79

Caddo 12
Catlin, George 42
Celts 27, 51, 53, 63, 74
Cherokee 2, 82
Cheyenne 58
Choctaw 2
Chippewa *see* Ojibway
chakras 8, 66
child-rearing 80–81
clans 12, 27, 50

Columbus, Christopher 1
constellations 19–23, 48
Corte-Real, Gaspar 2
coup-counting 77
Coyote 27
Crazy Horse 32, 33
Crazy Owl society 79
creation myths
   Apache 11
   Caddo 12
   Hopi 7–11, 13
   Iroquois 12
   Lakota 5–7, 13
   Navajo 11–12
   Ojibway 12
Creek 59, 82
Crow Dog, Leonard 71
Crowfoot 76–7
Custer, General George 3

dance 58, 81
democracy 81–2
Directions 12–16, 26, 32, 50, 58
diseases, European 2
divination 34–35
dreams 31–32

Eddy, John 20
elders, respect for 79–80

Fallen Star 20–23, 46
fire, sacred 58–59
Flathead 79
flood myths 5, 10, 12, 60

Geronimo 3, 18, 77
Ghost dance 3, 70–1
giveaway ceremony 54, 69–70, 72
Grandfathers, Six *see* Directions

Index

Harney Peak 18, 20
heyokas 31–32
Hinduism 10
holistic thinking 83
homosexuality 79
honesty 74–75
Hopi
    creation myth 7–11, 38
    Directional colours 16
    kiva 38
    migrations 1, 9–11
    páho 41
    rituals 46, 48–49, 50, 58, 63–66
    spirits 27
hospitality 81
Hunka ceremony 68–69
Huron 34, 54

Iktome 27
incest, feared 50
Internet 84
Inyan 5–7, 10, 13
Iroquois 12, 39

Jackson, President Andrew 2
Joseph, Chief 74–75

Kicking Bear 70, 71
Kootenai 79
Koyukon 28

Lakota
    dreams, obligations arising from 31–32
    myths 5–7, 11, 46, 60
    resistance to whites 3
    rites 49–50, 50–1, 51–54, 58, 67–69, 70–71
    star lore 20–23, 51
    symbolism, use 37–38, 42
    tipis 37–38
    visions 32–33
    Wounded Knee massacre 3–4, 71
land rights 76–7
languages, Native American 1, 29, 31; *see also* Micmac, language
Little Big Horn battle 3, 32, 78

Mandan 2
Másaw 9, 64
medicine wheel 16–17; *see also* Big Horn Medicine Wheel

Micmac
    Directional colours 16
    language 13, 29, 31, 59, 80
    myths 60–61
    smudging 59
    symbolism 30
midwifery 47–48
migration to American continent
    European 2
    Native American 1, 10–11
Milky Way 51
months, naming 29
morality, attitude to 73–74
music 58

names, personal 33
nature, respect for 27–29
Navajo
    Directional colours 16
    divination 34
    healing 39–41
    homes 37
    hospitality 81
    myths 11–12
    rites 48, 49
    sacred sites 16, 18–19, 37
New Holy, Alice 30
Nez Percé 74
Niman Kachina 64, 66
Nootka 28

Ojibway 12
Osage 30, 37

Papago 33
páho 41
parfleches 39–41
Pima 33
pipe, sacred 57–58, 59–61
Pleiades 19, 20–23, 65
Powamu 64, 66
pow-wows 78, 81
property ownership 76–77

quillwork 30

Red Cloud 23
reincarnation 46–48, 51, 80
reservations 4, 83
rites of passage
    birth 46–48

childhood 48–49
funeral 51–54
marriage 49–51
origins of 45
puberty 49–50
ritual
   artefacts 57–58
   location 57
   purpose 56–7
   role-playing 57
Running Eagle 79

sacred sites 17–19; *see also* ritual, location
salamander 48
Sams, Jamie 34–35
seasons 63–66
Seneca 34–35, 39
Short Bull 70, 71
Sioux
   meaning of name 4
   see also Lakota
Sitting Bull 3, 32, 33
Skan 6
smudging 59
snakes, ceremonial use 66
Sotuknang 7–9
soul-keeping 52–54, 60
Soyál 65–66
Spanish colonialists 2
Spider (Man) 27
Spider (Woman) 7, 9
spirit world 25–27
Squanto 2
stars, observation of 19–23
storytelling 84
Sundance 6, 26, 50, 67–68, 71–72
swastika 10, 16–17
sweatlodge 61–3
symbolism
   hogan 37
   attitude to 36–37
   parfleche 39
   tipi 37–38

Taiowa 7, 9
Tatanka 26–27
Thunder Beings 14, 31–32
time, attitudes to 29–31
tipi 37–38, 53
Tlinglit 54
To Win (Blue Woman) 47
tobacco, used ritually 59, 61
Tsimshian 54
turtle 12, 48

umbilical cord 46, 48
underworld 11, 64

Venus, planet 15
veterans, war 78, 81
Vikings 1
vision quest 32–33, 35

Wakinyan 14, 31–32
warrior code 77–78
Waziah 15
White Buffalo Calf Woman 15, 60, 61
winter counts 30
Wohpe, compared with Aphrodite 6
women, role of 78–9
Wounded Knee massacre 3–4
Wovoka 70–1
Wúwuchim 64

Young Chief 75
Yuma 52

Zuni 19

A BEGINNER'S GUIDE

Timeless Wisdom of the Celts

Steve Eddy & Claire Hamilton

This book reveals the roots of ancient Celtic wisdom and gives practical advice on how to apply it to our everyday life: our relationships and sexuality; our family; home; work; health and spirituality.

Timeless Wisdom of the Celts investigates the cultural and historical context of a people who emerged around the 5th century BC. Steve Eddy and Claire Hamilton look at a wealth of examples, including:

- the Celts in history
- gods and goddesses
- the relationship of the Celts with nature
- the role of the hero
- the cycles of the season
- the Otherworld
- the arts
- myths and legends

The book shows how all of these topics relate to modern life, and continue to intrigue and inspire us.

A BEGINNER'S GUIDE

Timeless Wisdom of the Egyptians

Ron Bonewitz

Timeless Wisdom of the Egyptians reveal the roots of ancient Egyptian wisdom and gives practical advice on how to apply it to our everyday life: our relationships and sexuality; our family; home; work; health and spirituality.

This fascinating book investigates the cultural and historial context of a tradition that has influenced many civilizations for 5,000 years. Looking at a wealth of examples including the power of pyramids, beliefs about the afterlife, the soul, the heart-centre and Mother Earth. Ron Bonewitz explains how Egyptian symbolism and mystery still intrigue us and can teach us how to get in touch with ourselves.

Exercises at the end of each chapter bring us into personal harmony with the inner power of Egypt.